THE
DIGITAL
UTILITY

Using energy data to increase
customer value and grow your business

Wayne Pales

First published in 2018 by Grammar Factory Pty Ltd.

A catalogue record for this book is available from the National Library of Australia

NATIONAL
LIBRARY
OF AUSTRALIA

Printed in Australia by McPhersons Printing
Cover design by Designerbility
Book production and editorial services by Grammar Factory

Disclaimer

'Having known and worked with Wayne for the best part of a decade, I've been impressed by his passion and thirst for knowledge on everything to do with smart energy. He established collaborative discussions and initiatives with leading international utilities with the aim to transform Hong Kong to a world-leading smart city. Wayne always challenges the status quo with the objective to constantly improve. I greatly appreciate his intellect and perspective, which always left me in a better position to improve our business.'

Rick Truscott, Chief Operating Office
CLP Power, Hong Kong

'Wayne led the team that engineered South East Asia's first smart metering and demand-response program. The team went on to receive a number of awards in Hong Kong and the region. During Wayne's time working for me, I respected his unwavering belief that creating values with energy data is at the heart of improving the services to the people and businesses of Hong Kong.'

TF Chow, Chief Operating Officer,
CLP Power, Hong Kong (2013-2016)

'Wayne has provided us with insights on Smart Grid and Smart Meters. In particular, the practical application of policy, governance, and implementation.'

Loo Kok Seng, Senior General Manager – Sustainability and
Corporate Asset Management, Tenaga Nasional Berhad, Malaysia

'I first invited Wayne to lecture for us at the Asian Institute of Technology in 2016. Wayne is well respected in the region and brings an up to date, fresh perspective to utilities across Asia through the strategic leadership program he created and delivers for us at AIT. His experience in management, planning, design, and operations of state-of-the-art technologies adapted to local conditions has been invaluable to the success of our programs.'

Greg Chiu, Professor of Practice,
Asian Institute of Technology, Thailand

'I first met and worked with Wayne when he was the head of Smart Grid for a utility in Hong Kong back in 2012. We worked together on a forward-looking demand-response program for residential customers. In 2017, when I co-founded Positive Energy.Community, I immediately reached out to Wayne to become an advisory board member. Wayne has a unique understanding of the Asian and Pacific energy markets, and utility strategies. With Wayne, Positive Energy. Community has strengthened its team of A level advisors in order to change the energy industry leveraging blockchain technology.'

Nicolas Payen, COO & Co-Founder
Positive Energy.Community, Singapore

'With his broad industry experience, Wayne is able to articulate a clear vision of the big picture and ground it with a technical understanding of how to make all of the pieces work together.'

Paul Nelsen – Vice President Asia Pacific Electricity
at Itron, Singapore

'I met Wayne in 2012 when he was researching how to best introduce South East Asia's first Demand Response program. I've always been impressed with Wayne's passion for pushing industry boundaries to advance demand response in the region.'

Amit Narayan, Founder & CEO AutoGrid Systems, United States

'Wayne is an active member of the IOT Alliance Australia. His belief that open access to energy data will accelerate the transition to sustainable cities is helping shape the standards we are developing at the alliance.'

Mark Atkinson, Internet of Things Alliance Australia (IOTAA)

'I've had the pleasure of working closely with Wayne over several years as he has shown an ability to innovate and transform the traditional ways that utilities think about new energy services, digital technology and industry disruption. In particular, Wayne's deep understanding of the value proposition surrounding smart metering gives a unique blend of technical, commercial and practical business insights. Above all, Wayne can be trusted to remain fiercely independent in his views and is passionate about a cleaner, smarter and more efficient energy future.'

Adrian Clarke, Chief Executive Officer – South East Asia, Australia and New Zealand, Landis+Gyr

'Wayne is the go-to specialist on the Asian and Australian expo circuit for digital utility expertise – a highly sought after speaker with valued insights on smart energy innovation.'

Rod McLauchlan, Show Director,
Digital Utility EXPO & Innovations in Energy Services, Singapore

Contents

Introduction:
A strategic roadmap for the future

Our industry is undergoing an enormous transformation. We face regulatory uncertainty, preventing us from making long-term infrastructure investments with confidence. Policy decisions are hindering our ability to invest in a low-carbon economy. Consumer adoption of new energy technologies, such as rooftop solar, is changing the face of our industry. And new entrants are dramatically eating into our traditional revenue models.

As an executive of an electric utility, you are under pressure from a wide range of stakeholders to demonstrate value. You are under pressure from consumers, many of whom feel your organisation is out of touch with what they want and expect, so they turn to alternative energy solutions. You are under pressure from start-ups, which recognise that you are struggling to adapt to all the advances taking place behind the meter, and so they are delivering the products and services consumers want. (Behind-the-meter typically refers to energy technologies such as rooftop solar, battery storage and energy management systems that a utility does not own or operate.) You are under threat from regulators trying to inject greater competition into the market. Your shareholders continue to expect short-term returns, yet other stakeholder groups don't think you are doing enough to reduce your company's environmental footprint. You are also under pressure from yourself, as you have to decide which investments need to be made to ensure short-term performance, long-term success, and the ongoing survival of your company. To help your company not only survive but thrive and prosper – for years and years to come – you need a strategic roadmap, tailored to your company.

Every utility operates in a unique environment, influenced by the industry regulator, the community, its consumers, its ability to source power, its executive team and its legacy. All of these factors combine to create a lot of uncertainty, so what the utility of the future needs is flexibility. Whatever roadmap you lay down now, that roadmap will need to change course at some point. Technology is advancing too fast for it not to. Gone are the days of laying out a five-year plan and sticking to it. The utility of the future, regardless of regulatory structure, will be one part of an ecosystem where data and power are flowing in every direction, and where we measure success by the value we deliver to our customers.

Energy data is at the heart of a successful digital utility. Historically, a utility would typically read the energy consumption of a residential customer once every other month. That meant all we knew about our customers was how much energy they consumed once every two months. We had no idea when they were using that energy within that period, so we had no idea how an individual customer's energy use was impacting the performance of the electricity grid. Just ten years ago, with regard to customers' homes, there was not much activity behind the meter. There was very limited uptake of rooftop solar and local battery storage. Electric vehicles were something left to science fiction movies. And smart appliances, such as air conditioners that can connect to your home's wireless network, simply did not exist. Today, behind-the-meter technologies are being adopted at an increasing rate, massively changing the way they consume and generate electricity. The energy data that all this is creating is the lifeblood of a digital utility.

This book will help you, as an executive of an electric utility, develop a strategic roadmap for the future, and secure support from your key stakeholders to implement it. With this roadmap, your organisation will be empowered to combat the major threats it faces by helping you increase customer value and, as a result, create a sustainable, successful business. Without this roadmap, you'll struggle to survive in this increasingly competitive environment.

My quest to help utilities build smart cities

To understand why I wrote this book, and why I am committed to helping utility companies succeed, you first need to understand how a series of events reshaped my priorities. These events happened in relatively quick succession between 2014 and 2016.

Up until 2016, I had been living and working in Hong Kong for almost seven years. I worked for one of Asia's most respected and successful electric utilities. Everything in my professional life was going exceptionally well. I loved the company I worked for and the role I was performing. We were making a real difference piloting and introducing new products and services that would help the residents and businesses of Hong Kong conserve energy and save a bit of money. My team and I were winning awards, and a leading industry magazine had voted me one of the most influential people in smart energy. On a professional level, things were good.

My personal life was somewhat different. My daughter was born early in 2014. I struggled with the idea of bringing her up in one of the most polluted cities in the world. Hong Kong has rising cases of asthma and bronchial infections in children that are linked to increased air pollution. Every time she coughed or got a cold, I berated myself. I knew I wanted to return to Australia; it was just a case of when.

While all this was happening, I was thinking about the path I would take once I left Hong Kong. If you're familiar with Hong Kong, no doubt you will have heard of Happy Valley, home of horse racing. Perhaps you've heard of The Chapel, an old English-style pub. Unfortunately, this pub no longer exists. However, I used to visit it regularly with Phil Stone, an industry colleague who has always worked for vendors (trying to sell technologies and services into utilities), whereas I have always worked for utilities (focusing on delivering energy services to consumers). We would talk at length about the challenges the industry was facing, based on our different perspectives. In mid-2015, during one of these discussions, we explored the threats to utilities as a result of the consumer-led adoption of behind-the-meter technologies such as rooftop solar. We explored how we could turn these threats into opportunities for utilities that leveraged the energy data generated by smart meters. The more we looked into this, the more we became convinced that utilities had the expertise and resources to use energy data to help their communities address the environmental issues we face.

We decided to create a company focused on helping electric utilities use energy data to increase customer value and deliver business growth. Our belief was simple: There is increasing consumer adoption of behind-the-meter technologies such as rooftop solar, electric vehicles, battery storage, and the connected home. Consumers are on this journey regardless of what their utility providers do. We believe that if we can help utilities leverage energy data, they can deliver services and products that position them at the heart of what is an inevitable transformation to a sustainable way of living.

Later in 2015, we formed The Chapel Group, and in early 2016 I moved to Melbourne, committed to working with electric utilities globally to help people get access to sustainable energy and to stop unnecessary consumption.

Almost two years after returning to Australia, I am proud to publish a book that introduces a framework that I believe can help utilities play a significant role in the move to a low-carbon society.

I wrote this book in two parts. The first part looks at the utility of the future. That is, what I believe we need to aspire to, and the changes in thinking that are required if we are to get there. This includes four basic industry insights that even the most successful utility companies have a tendency to overlook.

In the second part of the book, I guide you through my six-step EN-ERGY framework. This framework is a flexible roadmap that will enable you to effectively collaborate with your stakeholders, keep your team abreast of the latest advancements in technology, build a partner ecosystem to deliver the outcomes you need, and start thinking like a start-up; continuously testing, learning and course-correcting. Part 2 will share exactly how you can achieve all of this by following the six-step ENERGY framework.

Finally, I offer up my thoughts on where to from here. Governments around the world are battling with the challenge of how to grow their economies while also reducing their impact on the environment and improving the lives of their citizens. With the mass urbanisation of our planet, people are moving away from rural living to urban living, so the focus is on our cities. In China, for example, the percentage of people living in cities rose from thirteen per cent to 40.4 per cent between 1950 and 2005. It is predicted to rise to 60.3 per cent by 2030. Governments are turning to technology to address these challenges and, as a result, the term 'smart city' has emerged. Smart use of electricity is the foundation of a smart city, so utilities around the world play a very important role in their country's journey to introduce smart cities.

This book is written based on my personal journey, with the EN-

ERGY framework maturing over the last seven years. My hope is that this book will help you navigate the major threats in front of you today to help your utility become a more successful, more sustainable company.

Let's get started.

PART ONE:

THE UTILITY OF THE FUTURE

Chapter 1:
Striving for a competitive monopoly

For a long time, our industry has enjoyed protection from competition. We have been a monopoly, but this is changing. Competition is entering our market in a variety of ways, such as changes in regulations, the introduction of new technologies, and changing attitudes of energy consumers. In this chapter, I'll reveal insights on how to survive in this increasingly competitive environment, including the secret to becoming a competitive monopoly, and how to face the inevitable disruption occurring in our industry. With these insights, you'll be better positioned to understand and implement my six-step ENERGY framework.

Surviving in an increasingly competitive environment

In recent years, regulations have changed in certain parts of the world, introducing competition at different stages in the supply chain. In Australia, for example, we have seen wholesale markets emerge, bringing competition to the generation of electricity. More recently, some wholesale markets, such as California, are supporting the introduction of demand response through the conservation of energy as opposed to its generation. In countries such as the UK, Australia, New Zealand and, more recently, Japan, we have seen retail markets emerge to introduce competition, so consumers have a wider choice of energy retailers.

In the UK, independent distributors can manage private networks (such as microgrids, shopping centres and apartment blocks) instead of the primary distributor. The same is possible in Australia, although there it is referred to as an embedded network. Embedded networks are a fascinating area to watch. Examples of a private or embedded network are caravan parks, shopping centres, industrial parks and apartment buildings. These are a collection of premises that are likely to have facilities such as waste, water and energy managed by a central body. The private network concept is simply the next step, whereby those central management bodies can now take over the role of the network business to ensure the power within its premises is being delivered safely, securely and reliably. They also record the energy being consumed by each individual premise and can bill the customer for that usage. The private or embedded network has an arrangement with its utility to buy power from the grid on behalf of all the premises it oversees.

There is exponential growth in apartment living in many parts of the world. Even in Australia, with its vast open spaces, one in five people were living in apartments as of 2016, compared to one in seven back in 1991. If these apartments became embedded networks, managed by independent operators, there would be grave consequences for the incumbent utilities (both retailers and network businesses). The retailer would no longer be able to sell its electricity at retail rates to all the people living in apartment buildings. Instead, the embedded network would buy from the retailer at reduced wholesale rates, and it would make a profit from selling to the people living in the apartments. Distributors' revenue would decline because they would no longer be responsible for ensuring the electricity was supplied to each premise, but just to the main supply point of that embedded network. In fact, I believe that, regardless of the regulatory structure, the embedded network concept may become the most disruptive threat to many utilities around the world once regulators become familiar with the benefits this offers to the broader community. Imagine apartment blocks that already have people managing the facilities of their residents. If the embedded network operator could buy the energy at wholesale rates from their utility, then sell it to the residents of the apartment block at a rate lower than that being offered by the utility, the consumer is better off. To provide the customer with choice and control, the regulator could allow the resident to choose to receive energy services from either the utility or the embedded network operator.

New energy and communication technologies are creating competition in what is called 'behind-the-meter'. These are technologies the consumer is buying to take back control and give themselves more choice. These technologies include rooftop solar, battery storage, electric vehicles, and smart devices in the home, such as smart thermostats and smart air conditioners. Rooftop solar continues to grow, and will materially disrupt many traditional energy markets around the world. For example, in Australia more than one in five houses have solar panels installed. With rooftop solar established, we see the focus shift to local energy storage. We see a similar trend with solar energy storage as we saw with solar. Sticking with our example in Australia, a poll from the Climate Council of 2000 households found sixty-eight per cent of households already using solar are considering buying battery storage.

A multi-government program, called the Electric Vehicle Initiative, is targeting at least thirty per cent of new vehicle sales to be electric by 2030. On the surface, this is a good thing, as all these new car owners will no longer fill up their car with petrol or diesel. Instead, they will plug it into an electric power source, creating a new revenue source for utilities. However, electric vehicles also introduce threats to the power grid. The power grid is designed to always deliver power when it is needed. As we see a significant uptake of electric vehicles, their demand for power as they are placed on charge may place stress on the grid. Think about the scenario where lots of people are returning home from work around the same time. Those people place their electric vehicle on charge, go into their house, turn on the air conditioner and the TV, and start cooking dinner. All of these activities are demanding power from the grid at the same time.

Electric vehicles can also be used as battery storage. In the same way stationary battery storage can be used, technologies are being developed to leverage the electric vehicle's battery to reduce a consumer's reliance on the grid and optimise their energy use.

The connected home, whereby household devices and appliances are connected to a home's wireless network and controlled by a central hub, is still an emerging concept. For example, the locks on your doors, your lights, your entertainment system, and your heating and cooling may all be connected to a central hub via your home's wireless network. You can have an application running on your smartphone that allows you to monitor usage of these devices, and also remotely control them. For example, the system knows you have left the house, as it knows the location of your phone. It tells you if you have left the air conditioner on, asking if you would like it turned off. You confirm 'yes', and it turns the air conditioner off. This technology is in its very early stages, but consumer electronic giants are releasing products such as Apple's HomePod, Amazon's Echo and Google's Home, which have the potential to connect all smart devices within a home and remotely control them through a single application. In fact, the technology is moving beyond a smartphone application to a virtual assistant, where you can talk to these devices and they will execute your commands. The connected home, along with enhanced energy management, is the next battlefield for these consumer electronic behemoths.

In short, competition is increasing due to a combination of regulatory change, new energy technologies and changing consumer attitudes. In order to survive and prosper in this increasingly competitive environment, you need to be able to offer your customers something they want that others can't. In other words, you need to become a competitive monopoly.

The secret to becoming a competitive monopoly

If you're unfamiliar with this term, let me start by giving you some examples. I'll focus on the technology industry, since this is where you'll find the most recognisable competitive monopolies. For example, there are loads of social networking sites, yet Facebook continues to dominate. Similarly, retail giant Amazon competes in many verticals, yet it dominates its rivals and is often heralded as the world's online store. Meanwhile, Google competes with other search engines, yet it continues to dominate this space. All of these companies are competitive monopolies. They operate in a competitive market, and yet they have some secret that makes everyone use them.

It is this goal of becoming a competitive monopoly that I believe utilities need to aspire to. Regardless of other offerings available in the market, if you have a competitive monopoly, energy consumers will choose you. Today, most consumers are looking for ways to move away from a relationship with their utility. They are certainly not looking to build stronger relationships with utility companies. But there is a way to change that, with a secret you already possess.

The secret that your utility has, which no-one else has, is access to your energy data. This data is your secret. This data can allow you to position yourself as a critical part of the energy transformation and, I argue, as an essential element of a country's ambitions to introduce smart cities. I am not suggesting you hoard the data. Quite the opposite, in fact. (Later in the book, I talk about the need for you to make the data available to others.) I am encouraging you to think of your company as an Airbnb or an Uber, both of which bring together consumers and providers. You can become a two-way energy marketplace, where you facilitate the movement of electrons and data. Where you bring together energy consumers and service providers, all leveraging the energy data that you manage.

By doing this, you can differentiate yourself from all other players entering the market. You can offer something no-one else can. Even if, in years to come, others can provide this same service, it will be too late. You will have established a partner and consumer network that cements your leadership position. You will have become a competitive monopoly.

But before you can become a competitive monopoly, you need to understand what is going on around you.

Facing the inevitable disruption

As a senior executive of an electric utility, you are always being reminded of the disruption taking place within the industry. You face regulatory uncertainty, which means you can no longer make long-term infrastructure investments with confidence. Policy decisions are hindering your ability to invest in behind-the-meter solutions. Consumer adoption of new energy technologies, such as rooftop solar and battery storage, is impacting revenue and changing how networks are managed. And to top it all off, new entrants –

in areas such as private or embedded networks – will dramatically eat into the traditional revenue models of many utilities.

All of us have been battling with how to respond to this inevitable disruption. We know we must face the disruption head on, and increase the lifetime value of our customers to keep our businesses afloat, but there are often competing priorities. We still need to 'keep the lights on' (no pun intended) and run the business. We need to satisfy short-term demand from our shareholders and deliver healthy returns. And we need to justify why we are making investments in future opportunities that have an uncertain outcome and may, in the short term, reduce our revenue, increase our operational costs, or both.

Everyone I talk to agrees the future of our industry is uncertain. There are strong views put forward by a variety of experts, often with opposing positions. For example, some experts do not believe demand response will play a significant role in their country's future energy mix, while others feel it will play a major role. Opposing views also apply to the adoption and impact of the connected home, of electric vehicles and, to a lesser extent, rooftop solar and local battery storage. Given all of the conflicting opinions and advice, how can we be expected to make the right investment decisions? It can feel safer to remain unchanged until the fog clears and we have more certainty. The problem with this approach is that the fog will not clear for many years, if ever.

So, we need to look for lead indicators that can help us navigate this uncertainty and help build digital smart cities of the future. These lead indicators are what I call industry truths. These industry truths are the reality that is happening around us, regardless of what we, as electricity professionals, decide to do. We must take notice of this reality and allow it to inform the investment decisions we make. These truths need to be at the heart of the set of hypotheses we need to develop (which I discuss in a later chapter) and our journey to smart cities.

I believe there are six industry truths that we, as an industry, need to factor into our investment planning decisions in the coming years. I will reveal them to you in the next chapter, along with something called the Energy Trilemma. But first, here's a quick summary of the key points discussed in Chapter 1:

- Competition is entering our market in a variety of ways, such as changes in regulations, the introduction of new technologies, and changing attitudes of energy consumers.

- To survive in this increasingly competitive environment you need to become a competitive monopoly, whereby you offer your customers something – a secret – that no-one else has.

- The secret is your energy data. This data can allow you to position yourself as a critical part of the energy transformation.

- Before you can do this, you need to understand what is going on around you. There are six industry truths you need to factor into your investment planning decisions in the coming years.

Chapter 2:
Facing the truth ... and your biggest challenges

Just five to ten years ago, depending where you are in the world, external forces affecting the energy market were relatively predictable and constant. Energy demand would increase in line with the economy. The profile of a customer's energy consumption was also largely predictable. Before behind-the-meter technologies were widely available, it was relatively easy for a utility to model the energy use of a typical premise based on its own historical data. Investment planning in the grid was relatively straightforward.

By contrast, planning network investments today is no longer straightforward. Now we must take a serious look at what is going on around us, and have this inform our decisions.

So what is going on around us? I believe there are six industry truths we need to factor into our investment planning decisions in the future. In this chapter, I'll provide an overview of each industry truth. I'll also identify eight major challenges facing utility executives, and how the industry truths can help in addressing those challenges.

Six industry truths you cannot ignore

There are six truths currently facing the energy industry:

1. New energy technology is getting cheaper, physically smaller and more efficient.
2. Everything is becoming connected.
3. Growth of data is increasing insights into companies and consumers.
4. Energy consumers are striving for greater choice and control.
5. Energy consumers expect simplicity.
6. Reducing the impact we have on our planet is an increasingly important part of investment decisions.

How we decide to interpret these truths is up to us, but we cannot ignore them.

Truth 1: New energy technology is getting cheaper, physically smaller and more efficient

Whatever unit you use to compare, new energy technology is getting cheaper, physically smaller and more efficient. Solar technologies are the best example of this, with battery storage following suit. The more people buying solar and battery storage, the more investment will be made to make them better and cheaper, and on the cycle goes. This is important for utilities to observe, as this pattern means consumers are likely to purchase these new energy technologies at increasing rates as they become more affordable to a larger section of the population. Remember, left alone, the adoption of behind-the-meter technologies such as solar and battery storage means future revenue from energy sales will be both unpredictable and reduced.

In the not-too-distant future, we will see solar technology extend beyond rooftop panels to solar pavements, solar paint, solar tiles, and so on. High-rise apartment buildings – often placed in the 'too hard basket' when it comes to introducing solar energy and storage – are now within reach. Projects have emerged that introduce solar and storage into multi-residential complexes. These projects are breaking down the traditional barriers to entry, where solar and storage would only be feasible when installed in a single household.

I believe the connected home will experience the same trend. Amazon, Google, Microsoft and Apple are all releasing products that consumers can purchase so they can connect all of their home's smart devices to a central hub. This hub provides the ability to manage all of these devices and appliances from a single application. Let me give you an example. Today you can purchase smart locks that take a video recording of who rings your doorbell. The smart lock knows when you are not at home and can tell you whether the house is locked. Now imagine a smart air conditioner. Again, it can know when you are away from home and notify you that it is still on. Other devices around the home, including lighting, entertainment systems, and heating and cooling, are becoming smart as well. The challenge is that the data they are generating, and the means of controlling the devices, are all in isolation from one another. For every smart device, you need a smartphone application. The concept behind these central hubs is that they connect all of these devices and appliances into one place, so you have a single view of all your activity and the ability to control them all from one platform. A further interesting development is that these devices have what is called a digital virtual assistant. In the case of Apple, this is Siri. So rather than open your iPhone Home application, in the future you can say, 'Hey, Siri. Make me warmer,' and the heating will turn on. In fact, these technologies are also looking at ways to introduce artificial intelligence, or AI. AI learns your behaviour over time and can make adjustments to the appliances around your home, based on what it thinks you will like, without you doing anything. Again, why do utilities need to take note of the move to a connected home? Because smarter devices in the home means customers will reduce unnecessary energy use, so a utility's revenue will go down.

Everywhere we look, new energy technologies are becoming more accessible to households and businesses. Utilities recognise overall that their energy sales are likely to decrease as consumers generate and store their own energy, as well as optimise their use of it. Therefore, forward-thinking utilities are looking at ways to partner with the consumer. They are coming up with services, such as demand response programs, that help them reduce their costs of managing the grid. They are also coming up with new services that help them create new revenue sources, such as selling, installing and operating rooftop solar, home energy storage and connected-home solutions.

Truth 2: Everything is becoming connected

There is an enormous amount of hype associated with the Internet of Things, a term first coined by Kevin Ashton in 1999. The term has been around for many years, yet there is still no globally agreed-upon definition. The *Oxford English Dictionary* defines the Internet of Things as 'the interconnection via the Internet of computing devices embedded in everyday objects, enabling them to send and receive data.' On the grid side, we see deployments of smart meters and other sensors across the network. The idea is to generate much more granular and timely insights into operations and consumer behaviour so that we can make more accurate and timely business decisions. As these technologies generate more data, and generate it more frequently, shipping it all from where it was created (such as a customer's home) all the way back to a utility's computer systems – to analyse the data, make a decision, and then send a command all the way back to the customer's home – has become increasingly inefficient. With electricity, decisions need to be made instantaneously. So now we are seeing data-generating technologies, such as smart meters, not just recording energy consumption but, thanks to an inbuilt computing power, analysing that data and taking action without first sending the data to the utility and waiting for a decision to be made. This is known as edge computing or distributed intelligence. An example of this is with electric vehicles. Imagine you live in a neighbourhood where people are starting to buy electric vehicles. They all come home from work and plug those vehicles in at the same time. The surge in power demand may be too much for that part of the grid to manage, which results in many people losing power until the utility can identify the problem. With edge processing, the grid knows the maximum power demand it can manage. If it notices more demand by way of an electric vehicle being plugged in, it can prevent that vehicle from receiving power until more power becomes available when someone else unplugs something. This may not seem like a great outcome for that electric vehicle owner, but it's far better than lots of people losing power. This move to edge processing means utilities can now leverage technology to gain insight and take action, in near real-time, anywhere on their network.

In addition to equipment on the grid becoming more connected, we are also seeing home appliances, such as smart air conditioners and smart thermostats, connecting to the internet.

As mentioned earlier, we are seeing a move by major consumer technology players – such as Apple, Amazon, Google and Microsoft – to play a vital role in connecting all in-home smart devices to a central hub. This allows them to view their activity, and control these devices and appliances, remotely from one smartphone application. This will result in greater convenience for the consumer, as well as reducing unnecessary energy usage. Every aspect of the home and power grid is becoming connected, which has huge implications for utilities and consumers alike. More connectivity means more data, enabling companies to gain greater insights into their customers' habits and desires. This is outlined in more detail in Truth 3.

Truth 3: Growth of data is increasing insights into companies and consumers.

The more we deploy connected technologies, the more data becomes available to consume. This data, often referred to as big data, will enable organisations to gain levels of insight into their company's performance and consumer behaviour never seen before.

Let me give you an example. In utilities, we see the rapid adoption of condition-based maintenance. Condition-based maintenance is where new sensors on equipment are generating enormous amounts of data in near real-time about the health of the equipment used to manage the electricity network. This data is analysed by the utility, enabling it to predict when failures will occur before they actually do. This allows the utility to replace or repair a piece of equipment before it fails and impacts the performance of the grid. Prior to condition-based maintenance, a utility would manage equipment through time-based maintenance, whereby it would schedule a piece of equipment to be assessed or replaced. There are problems with this approach: equipment may fail before you are due to assess it; you may replace equipment that was perfectly fine to run for many more years; and you incur costs of assessing equipment that may not need assessing. All up, condition-based maintenance reduces the cost of operating as well as the performance of the grid.

On the consumer side, insights from the enormous amounts of energy data now being recorded can be used to deliver new and improved services to consumers. For example, in an environment where a consumer can select their energy retailer, you may want to ensure your customer is on the most suitable tariff so they do not leave you for another offer. For a network business, you may identify consumers you can engage to reduce energy consumptions at certain times of the year when your network is under stress. This can prevent you from having to upgrade your network, and allows you to keep price rises at bay. For these reasons, securing advanced analytical capabilities, whether through partnering with an external provider or by developing them in-house, is key if you want to become a competitive monopoly and a leader in the use of smart technology.

Truth 4: Energy consumers strive for choice and control.

Consumers don't like being told what they can and cannot do. They want to have a choice, and they want to have control over their decisions. In Australia, we can see this happening with rooftop solar, which has been adopted by one in five houses. A poll by the Climate Council in Australia found that sixty-eight per cent of those with rooftop solar are considering buying energy storage solutions. These energy consumers will reduce their reliance on the grid, and have far greater choice and control over who they get their energy from in the future and how much they pay for it. This industry truth can, at times, conflict with another industry truth, and that is the desire for simplicity. Often, utilities create such a wide and varied range of products that customers become overwhelmed and frustrated, and, as a result, seek to take more control of the decision-making process. In comparison, some consumers feel like they have no choice at all. In many parts of the world, such as Australia, the drive to go 'off grid' (not using or depending on public utilities for the supply of electricity) comes about as a result of the consumer feeling they are locked in and that they have no good choices available to them. Currently, these off-grid investments are coming in the form of solutions such as rooftop solar, battery storage and the connected home, and aim to reduce reliance on the utility. The next step in this journey is for a customer to sign up to a service that can help them optimise their energy use. With advanced analytical capabilities, services are emerging that automate the process of helping the customer determine when to buy power from the grid, when to reduce their energy consumption, and when to sell power to the grid. As we head down this path, utilities need to understand that consumers will gain greater choice and control. Consumers will no longer rely on you for their energy – you now need to earn the right to provide services to them.

Technology has advanced to the point where consumers can now trade excess energy with others in their community. For example, someone may want to purchase electricity from their child's school, their local church or their community centre, as a way of supporting these organisations. They may want to donate their excess energy to others. Or, they may be able to source electricity at a lower cost than the utility can provide it. While outside the scope of this book, when there is widespread adoption of what is called peer-to-peer energy trading, the role of the utility will have to change significantly to manage the millions of micro-transactions occurring between households selling electricity and those that are buying.

Truth 5: Energy consumers expect simplicity.

The evolution of consumer electronics continues to demonstrate that people no longer take the time to study how things work. As Elon Musk famously said, 'Any product that needs a manual to work is broken.' Consumers expect solutions to be intuitive and take as few steps as possible. Think of any recent personal-use technology purchase such as a television, a game console or a smartphone. The set-up process is simple and intuitive, in the sense that you do not need to study large instruction manuals. The growth in smart devices for the home shows that, when it comes to electricity, people want to have 'set and forget' solutions. What I mean by the term 'set and forget' is that they want to set up the device once, and then trust it will optimise their energy use with the minimal amount of involvement from them. People want to lead the lifestyle they choose, in the most cost-effective manner, with the smallest environmental impact possible – all without having to take action. What this means is that we can expect to reach a point where technologies in the home are optimising energy usage on behalf of the consumer. This optimised use of energy will result in reduced energy sales for utilities.

There are two reasons we need to be mindful of this move to simplicity. First, there is a lot of electricity being used in people's homes unnecessarily. They have devices running when they don't need to. They have them running harder than they should, which means they are drawing more power. They are using appliances that are less energy efficient than they could be. With the move to smarter devices – where the device, not the consumer, makes the decision and takes action – we can expect energy sales to drop.

We also need to be mindful of this trend when trying to sell customers our own products and services. For customers to want to buy energy services from us, there needs to be a clear and simple value proposition. The technology (if there is any involved) needs to be simple for them to install, and the ongoing service needs to be as invisible to them as possible. We are now competing with consumer electronic giants, telcos, and many other organisations that are years ahead of us in their experience selling to consumers in very competitive markets.

Truth 6: Reducing the impact we have on our planet is an increasingly important part of investment decisions.

The amount they pay for their electricity is still, in the vast majority of cases, the consumer's primary concern. However, what I have been seeing is a growing number of consumers who, in addition to cost considerations, want to partner with organisations that provide 'green' energy, and are active in giving back to the community. Professors Christine Horne and Emily Kennedy published a study in the journal *Energy Policy* that showed many Americans would prefer to power their homes with wind, solar and other forms of renewable energy if given the option.

The problem with only focusing on the traditional, price-sensitive consumer is that it becomes a race to the bottom where nobody wins. Focusing solely on driving out costs and meeting the immediate demands of the majority of your customers will result in missed opportunities, and your company will eventually be surpassed by new entrants and alternative solutions.

Addressing your challenges to get ahead

The industry truths can be thought of as lead indicators, or predictive measurements that can influence change. Much like the 'canary in the coalmine' concept, lead indicators provide an early warning system as to what changes are coming and when they may occur.

We can use lead indicators to tackle some of the greatest challenges we face as the leaders of utility companies, including regulatory uncertainty, market deregulation, and so on. Here is a brief overview of eight industry challenges we must face.

Industry challenge 1: Regulatory uncertainty

Regulatory uncertainty comes about as policymakers themselves are struggling to design structures and policies that can effectively govern all market participants to work together to deliver on what the United Nation's World Energy Council calls the World Energy Trilemma.

The Energy Trilemma refers to the need to ensure the supply of electricity meets three core needs:

1. **Energy Security:** The ability of a country to source and deliver the physical energy required to power its businesses and citizens' homes, and deliver it to consumers in a safe and reliable manner.
2. **Energy Equity:** This ensures everyone within that country can access electricity, and do so in the most affordable way.
3. **Energy Sustainability:** The ability to deliver the energy in a manner that has the least impact on the environment, while still achieving the first two goals.

Regardless of whether a country has one integrated utility responsible for the end-to-end delivery of electricity, or has been disintegrated and has many parties involved in the value chain, the Energy Trilemma holds firm. Whether you are a technology start-up or a policymaker, you are making decisions based on the Energy Trilemma. Any decision you make must eventually support all three parts of the Energy Trilemma. There can be a heavier focus on one aspect over another, but all three must be covered if you want to ensure success.

The struggle to design structures and policies that can effectively govern market participants to deliver on the Energy Trilemma creates a great deal of regulatory uncertainty for utilities. This regulatory uncertainty impacts utilities' ability to make long-term investment decisions with confidence.

Industry challenge 2: Market deregulation

Where a regulator is exploring options to introduce competition, it injects uncertainty into the market. Creating a wholesale market – where generators would need to bid and compete on price, emissions and ramp-up time – would change the priority and investment decisions of an incumbent utility looking to expand its capacity. The introduction of retail competition would change how an incumbent utility would prioritise investments and even structure its business. Even in the 'poles and wires' business of transmission and distribution networks, incentives offered by a regulator – for non-utilities to introduce distributed generation and storage – will influence investment decisions. So, while regulators explore these options, a utility must decide where to place its focus and investment dollars. Often, the uncertainty leads to constant analysis, with the utility unable to commit to a particular investment plan and future direction.

Industry challenge 3: Diminished return on investment

Traditionally, utilities have been rewarded for ensuring they meet demand with adequate supply. As demand goes up, the utility would invest more in infrastructure to generate and transport that energy. The utility would typically receive a rate of return on the infrastructure assets it needs to invest in. Regulatory models that allow a utility to make a profit from encouraging customers to use less energy, and therefore allow them to invest less in infrastructure assets, are still not commonplace. This creates a natural tension where the utility knows it needs to focus on helping consumers conserve energy, especially at peak times, but is financially rewarded for doing just the opposite.

Industry challenge 4: Restrictions on innovation

Utilities have strict performance targets around safety and reliability of supply. Being risk-averse is part of the DNA of a utility. In the majority of cases, sufficient incentives are not in place to encourage the utility to innovate and take risks. This is tightly coupled with industry challenge number three (investment return). In many cases, a utility will deliver services such as energy audits and awareness campaigns to receive incentives laid out by its regulator. These incentives are often very limited in scale, so the utility does just enough to earn the incentive, but is not fully committed to scaling out those initiatives, as this would start to impact its core business. That impact would outweigh any incentives the utility receives from the regulator.

Industry challenge 5: Consumer adoption of new energy technologies

Whether it's to reduce environmental impact or cost, or just through frustration with their utility, more and more consumers are looking towards alternative technologies to meet their energy needs. This includes rooftop solar, battery storage, and smart devices such as the smart thermostat, which will eventually create a connected home. All of these have an impact on the traditional revenue model of a utility. There are a number of reasons why the consumer adoption of behind-the-meter technologies poses an increasing threat to utilities. Two of the main reasons are:

1. Without regulatory support, a utility needs to fund a path that delivers no financial reward. This is difficult, as the investment frameworks of many utilities do not support investments in areas that will not provide a demonstrable rate of return.

2. This is a new and fast-changing landscape. There is a lot of uncertainty, and the business case may not be able to show a clear return on investment. In fact, many of these investments will reduce energy consumption from the grid, especially at peak times, resulting in decreased energy sales and decreased infrastructure investment, and therefore a decreased rate of return.

Traditionally, energy companies stopped investments 'at the meter'. Anything behind the meter, which they did not own and control, was not their domain. In most cases, the utility did not have the necessary expertise to provide behind-the-meter technologies, so they would need to partner with an external provider. All of this is very new, and has an uncertain outcome. When you factor in the reasons outlined above, you can understand the hesitation to venture into a new and unknown area.

The knock-on effect – of consumers looking for energy solutions beyond their utility – means we are seeing new competition entering the market, including well-established players in other industries, as well as start-ups.

Industry challenge 6: Competition from established organisations in other industries

Telecommunications companies, or telcos, see the transformation happening in the energy sector as an opportunity. Telcos often operate in highly competitive environments, and have honed their skills in areas such as customer engagement and advanced analytics. They see the connected home as an extension to existing strategies, and also see their telecommunication networks as the key to connecting all these energy technologies. For example, Australia's largest telco, Telstra, has invested heavily in solar and storage, and offer connected-home products and services. All of these services are threats to incumbent utilities.

Consumer giants such as Apple, Google, Amazon and Microsoft are all entering the connected-home space. These tech and retail behemoths are making inroads into owning a hub in the home that connects and controls all smart devices. That means they will know the energy consumption of all devices and appliances, and have the ability to remotely control them. There are a range of services that can be created off the back of this, which will reduce a utility's revenue and its relationship with the customer.

Industry challenge 7: Competition from start-ups

When it comes to posing a threat to existing utilities, start-ups generally fall into three categories: The nimble start-up, the alternative start-up and the disruptive start-up.

1: The Nimble start-up

Companies such as EnerNOC (which was recently acquired for more than $300 million) spent years trying to work with utilities, but, for all the reasons outlined previously, eventually gained the traction they needed on their own. They re-positioned themselves to focus more heavily on other markets, such as large commercial and industrial customers. The issue with this is that, as wholesale markets mature and allow the bidding of the negawatt into the market, these companies become natural competitors. (Negawatt power is a theoretical unit of power, representing an amount of electrical power saved. The energy saved is a direct result of energy conservation or increased energy efficiency. The concept of a negawatt could influence a behavioural change in consumers by encouraging them to think about the energy they consume.)

Other examples that I would expect to emerge as major threats in the future are companies such as Tesla, with its static and mobile battery fleet, and Google's Nest, with its smart thermostat. Where utilities don't partner with them, these organisations will grow relationships directly with the consumer. These new entrants will bring under management a huge amount of negawatt power, which can be used to bid into the wholesale market. Other examples include solar and storage vendors, which will try to partner with utilities, but will happily go directly to the consumer if the utility is not prepared to partner with them.

2: The Alternative start-up

The second type of start-up is not necessarily competing with the energy company, but is providing services that erode the revenue of the energy company, along with their relationship with the consumer. There are start-ups that offer services around a range of demand-side services, such as energy efficiency, energy conservation, home automation, and even checking to ensure the customer's bill is accurate. Examples of this include Wattwatchers, which offers devices that measure the energy consumption of an individual household at very granular levels. This data is used to provide the consumer with advice on how they can reduce their energy consumption. Another example is Ambi Climate, a device that connects to air conditioners via its infra-red controller. The service not only allows the customer to remotely control the air conditioner, but it also has artificial intelligence that learns the behaviour of the owner and helps them maintain their preferred comfort levels as efficiently as possible. A utility's revenue is eroded as many of these services help the customer save energy. The utility's relationship with its customers is also weakened, as the customer now turns to these alternative service providers for their energy solutions, instead of the utility.

3: The Disruptive start-up

The third type of start-up includes those looking to make a disruptive play. Here are two examples:

1. **Peer-to-peer trading platforms**. These platforms allow consumers and businesses to sell excess energy to neighbours and peers. While they are still in their infancy, they will pick up pace as consumers become increasingly determined to buy and sell energy from different suppliers for a range of reasons (which are not always monetary). For example, people may choose to buy excess energy from their local church, community hall or school, at a slightly inflated price, if it helps give back to a cause they want to support.

2. **Virtual power plants (VPPs).** A VPP integrates several types of power sources to give a reliable overall power supply. These power sources are often a cluster of distributed generation systems, and are often orchestrated by a central authority. Think about this in the context of the move to embedded networks, where a private operator can manage the electricity network of an apartment block. Then consider projects where a system of communal solar and storage is created within apartment complexes, and, within those apartments, connected homes begin to emerge. This means residents would be able to reduce their reliance on power from the grid. The private operator could engage the utility and insist on wholesale prices, as it represents all the customers in its apartment block. Eventually, that apartment block could become a virtual power plant where the aggregated excess energy is bid into the wholesale market.

Regardless of whether your utility is in a regulated or deregulated environment, these start-ups will change the shape of the future energy landscape, and this is a real threat to you as an incumbent utility.

But it doesn't stop there. There's one more major challenge, or dilemma, you'll have to face if you want to survive.

Industry challenge 8: Making poor investment decisions

Every day, you face enormous pressure to keep the lights on, so to speak. With finite financial and human resources, and the limited brainpower of executives, there are only so many initiatives that can be invested in at any one time if they are to be successful. More often than not, those initiatives with a clear and immediate return on investment will be approved, leaving investments in future opportunities to fall by the wayside.

Even where funds are available, it can be very difficult to justify investments where you cannot guarantee outcomes. On another level, you may be personally incentivised to invest in initiatives that demonstrate an ability to increase revenue or reduce costs. It is quite rare for people within a utility to be financially incentivised based on investments that focus on learning, with no guaranteed outcome. In addition to this, while your shareholders want confidence in future returns, they are often not willing to sacrifice short-term returns to get there.

This often leads to investments in pilots (to test new ideas and concepts, and learn new things as a result) being shelved, or so scaled back that meaningful lessons cannot be learned.

These threats will impact a utility in different ways and at different times. As a utility executive, they could impact your ability to make the right investment decisions, which satisfy the short-term demands of consumers and shareholders, while also satisfying the long-term demands of the same stakeholders. It's a delicate balance – one that's becoming increasingly difficult to get right.

That brings us to the end of Chapter 2. By now, you should have a good understanding of the six immutable truths, or lead indicators, and how you can use them to combat the eight fears we face as an industry. In Chapter 3, we'll discuss how you can use these insights to help your company adapt and respond to the changes occurring within our industry. But first, here's a list of the key points discussed in Chapter 2:

- New energy technology is getting cheaper, physically smaller, and more efficient.
- Everything is becoming connected. More connectivity means more data, enabling companies to gain greater insights into their customers' habits and desires.
- Energy consumers are striving for greater choice and control, but also expect simplicity.
- Reducing the impact we have on our planet is an increasingly important part of investment decisions.

- The six industry truths can be thought of as lead indicators. We can use these lead indicators to tackle some of the greatest fears we have as the leaders of utility companies.
- There are eight major challenges utility executives face:
  - Regulatory uncertainty.
  - Market deregulation.
  - Diminished return on investment.
  - Restrictions on innovation.
  - Consumer adoption of new energy technologies.
  - Competition from established organisations in other industries.
  - Competition from start-ups.
  - Making poor investment decisions.

Chapter 3:
Focusing inwards to deliver outwards

Now that you have an understanding of the external factors shaping your company, you need to focus inwards. In short, you need to be clear on what sort of services you want to deliver to your customers, and why.

This may sound a bit overwhelming, but it's really very simple. At the heart of every decision, you must be able to answer 'yes' to this question: Will this service deliver customer value? That value may be direct, such as providing customers with a new service that helps them save money. It can also be indirect, such as introducing a service that helps you reduce your non-technical losses, which, in turn, reduces your cost to serve and therefore the rates you pass on to your customers.

It is all too easy for your 'innovation team' to get carried away with the latest and greatest technology, and lose sight of *why* you are interested in this technology in the first place. You have to know what services these new technologies will allow you to introduce, so you can understand the potential customer value and be able to discuss this with your various stakeholders in order to gain their support for the journey you are about to embark on. That's what we'll discuss in this chapter – how to prioritise services over technologies. I'll also explain the importance of performance metrics, and how to transition from 'gut feel' to data-led decision-making.

Staying focused on services over technologies

The best way to stay focused on services over technologies is to always ask yourself: What service am I trying to deliver, and why? This is a small but powerful question, especially in a utility, which will typically have a bunch of engineers and technologists. Too often, conversations jump straight to, 'How are we going to deliver this?' As soon as this happens, you have lost sight of what's important – your customers.

Let's take demand response as an example. (If you're not familiar with this term, demand response is where an organisation, such as a utility, has a need for a consumer to reduce their electricity usage during a specified period; usually for a few hours at a time, and only a few times a year.) The reasons why utilities call for demand response events vary. One reason is to reduce demand for power when the overall system is unable to generate enough power to satisfy demand. Without demand response, the utility would need to turn off power supply to customers to keep the whole system working.

So, your first step is to always be clear on why you want to provide a demand response service. With the example above, it is to defer investments in generation assets without creating power outages to customers, while also avoiding increased costs passed on to customers. Other reasons include deferral of investments in network assets, or so the utility can bid the demand response load into a wholesale market or use it as a backup option in emergency grid-stability situations. Understanding your reasons for wanting to provide such a service will help shape the service itself. Let's say we want customers to reduce their energy consumption during a time when the system cannot generate enough power to satisfy everyone. In this hypothetical example, these times of high demand – when the system is under stress – typically occur during summer, when people return home from work and turn on their air conditioners. Based on information from the weather bureau, you always know twelve hours in advance whether the system will be under stress. This is all vital information to know – way before you even think about the technology required to help reduce customers' energy consumption. Now that we know we have twelve hours to plan how we will reduce customers' energy consumption to avoid a blackout, we can design the right solution. In this example, it might simply be to send an email or an SMS to people on the morning before a high demand evening, asking them to reduce energy during the early evening. In return, you will give them a financial incentive. For this example, no advanced technologies are required.

It's important to know what service you will offer, and why. If you jump straight to the technical aspect, you may invest unnecessarily in myriad technologies to automatically reduce your customers' energy consumption, when a simple email or SMS was sufficient.

Let me give you another, simpler example. Let's say you want to buy a watch. Why do you want a watch? Is it to tell the time? To have a fashion accessory? To help with your fitness program? Once you know this, you can drill down into what services or features it needs to offer. If it is to help with your fitness, then you may want it to have a pedometer, a heart rate monitor, and so on. Once you know this, you can shop around for the right watch. You never care about *how* the watch works – your only concern is finding a watch that matches your needs and desires.

So, with that in mind, help your team become crystal clear on why they are exploring a certain area, and let that guide the services you want to deliver. By all means, speak to vendors who are trying to sell you products and services in the areas you are interested in, and understand all the various technologies and solutions out there so you know what's possible. But make sure the customer is always your key focus. Talk to your customers and find out what they're looking for. Is there a particular service or feature they'd like to see introduced? Why? (In Chapter 5, I'll reveal how to capture your customers' thoughts in a simple, straightforward way.)

Once you have clarity on the services you need to deliver and why, it becomes very easy to identify if solutions already exist, and, if not, who you should co-develop with. Jumping straight into the technological side of things may lead to success, but being clear on what you want to offer, and why, will resonate with customers on a much deeper level.

Knowing why you are embarking on this transformation journey, and what services you will deliver, is essential. However, it does not secure support, or funding. To get the necessary support from your stakeholders, you need to demonstrate that the investments you propose make sense. To do this, you need to be able to show improvement in existing performance and, ultimately, against key metrics such as the lifetime value of your customers. We'll discuss this in more detail in the section below.

Everything needs to be measured – no excuses

With the data that is becoming available to us through smart meters and other sensors, we no longer have any excuse for failing to measure the performance of our operations. With the advancements in analytics and associated modelling, there is also no excuse for failing to analyse our customers' energy consumption behaviour. We can increase our knowledge through the availability of energy data, including:

- Our cost to serve each customer. Cost to serve calculates the profitability of a customer account, based on the actual business activities and overhead costs incurred to service that customer. With energy data, we could better understand the consumption patterns of a particular customer to see if their demand for power is more than others, resulting in the utility needing to invest more in its infrastructure and pass those costs back to its customers.

- The lifetime value of our customers. This is a prediction of the net profit attributed to the entire future relationship with a customer, which can be enhanced with energy data.
- The drivers of technical and non-technical loss. This would enable utilities to address the root cause of various problems, reducing unnecessary revenue loss, where energy is being generated but can never be billed to anyone.

With the data that is now available to us, we need to revisit and extend what we are measuring. For example, we need to start looking at correlations, such as bill estimates that lead to billing enquiries and complaints. Or visits to our websites that lead to a phone call for a service the customer should have been able to find for themselves.

In short, everything needs to be measured, and there is no excuse not to. Old models also need to be revisited. For example, measuring outages is no longer reliant on the inaccurate practice of waiting for customers to call in to notify you of an outage, and then waiting for an engineer to confirm whether power has been restored. Instead, the meters tell you the exact times when power was lost and when it was restored. No longer should you develop segmentation models based solely on criteria such as location, energy consumed every two months, and various socioeconomic data to 'guess' people's consumption behaviour. Now we have access to very granular data.

For example, I can recall a time when we analysed the energy usage patterns of a set of customers that had historically been classified as having similar energy consumption patterns. Prior to smart meters, which record customer consumption every thirty minutes, we would record consumption once every two months when a meter reader physically visited the customer's house and read the meter. Because we had so little information on their energy usage, we had to classify customers based on characteristics such as where they lived, what type of property they lived in, and so on. When we analysed the energy data for these customers using smart meters, we were astonished to see just how different they were. For example, some customers used a lot of energy late at night on weekdays, while others used a lot of energy at weekends. In all, we had about eight very different usage patterns across a customer base that we used to classify as one group. With granular energy data, we were able to get a deep understanding of the energy consumption patterns of our customers, and more accurately determine which customers we wanted to reach out to and why. For example, if you are trying to reduce high energy demand on weekday evenings, there is no point spending time and money asking customers with very low usage during that period to further reduce their consumption. This would be a waste of money for the utility, and frustrating for the consumer. Insights from energy data can reduce your costs and help you influence customer behaviour by targeting the right customers.

Every service you are looking to introduce should have performance metrics established. Without this, you will not know if the investments you are making are worthwhile. If measurements are genuinely not in place, then you need to create them. (We'll discuss this in more detail in a later part of the book.)

You need to use metrics to remove the emotion from the work your team will be embarking on. For example, if you set up a stand-alone team to look at improving the way the business operates and the services it delivers to your customers, it will face obstacles. I recall a time when we were looking to capture metrics related to the total cost to the organisation of meter reading. When we compared the costs per read provided by the metering department with the modelling used by the finance department, they did not match in the slightest. The costs we were given were too low, so I spoke with the head of the metering department and explained the mismatch. Together with the finance department, we managed to uncover the real numbers. It turned out that the people we were talking to initially were concerned that, by giving us the real numbers, they may lose a significant portion of future funds should the project go ahead, so they decided to lower the unit cost. On reflection, this was as much our fault as theirs. We should have engaged the head of that department from the start, to get his support and help communicate what was required to the team. Being data-driven is the only way to overcome these barriers, as we were able to show the head of the department that the numbers we were initially given did not add up. It also kept everyone honest – and this works both ways. For example, there have been times when my team could not provide the metrics to support the recommended introduction of a service. We had to have a difficult conversation with the steering committee, outlining why we believed the service would be of value even though we could not quantify it.

At this point, I'd like to issue a word of caution. Using more so-phisticated technology and data will, at least initially, turn parts of your world upside down. You need to prepare for this, as many metrics are used to report performance externally and are tied to financial incentives and penalties. Let me give you an example, based on a personal experience regarding the accuracy of meter readings. With old meters, energy consumption was tracked based on the turn of the wheel inside a mechanical meter. They operate at a certain level of accuracy and, over time, they can slow down, recording less consumption than was actually used. Smart meters, on the other hand, will never slow down and are often in a higher accuracy class. Both meter types pass the regulatory standards, but they will give different results. On an individual customer level, the difference is minute. But if you aggregate it across all custom-ers, more units are able to be charged back to consumers, which, in theory, leads to a reduced tariff. A great outcome, right? The poten-tial threat here is: How would you manage the customer's percep-tion that, up until that point, they have not received accurate bills? The reality is that they have, but it's easy for people to perceive smart meters as more accurate than legacy meters.

Having said all that, the pros of using more sophisticated technol-ogy and data far outweigh the cons. I have been caught out too many times when I pushed forward in a particular direction, sim-ply because key stakeholders supported it. However, when out-comes were not quite as expected, we were exposed, as we had no data to back up the position. We were instead relying on 'gut feel', which is hugely problematic for any company trying to grow in a cost-effective way. This is something I discuss in more detail in the following section.

From gut feel to data-led decision-making

It is a big step for utilities to start using energy data to measure operational performance and customer behaviour. It is an even bigger step to move away from relying solely on gut feel and experience to becoming data-led in your decision-making.

Increasingly, utilities are embracing insights from the energy data they are collecting and using it to make decisions. According to Research and Markets, the size of the energy and utility analytics market is projected to grow from US$1.81 billion in 2016 to US$3.41 billion in 2021. That's a compound annual growth rate of 13.5 per cent. The large amount of energy data being recorded is often called big data, and refers to extremely large data sets that may be analysed computationally to reveal patterns, trends and associations, especially those relating to human behaviour and interactions. Utilities are moving away from solely relying on the experience and expertise that exists inside the heads of a few senior engineers. However, this is a hard transition. You are essentially replacing (if not entirely, then in large part) the tacit knowledge that only the most senior of engineers, with decades of experience, could know.

I recall a previous team I led, which had developed a very impressive model to predict critical peak demand using historical data, weather patterns and various algorithms. It went under extensive testing and had proved itself over and over again. We applied the model to the last five years of energy data and system peaks, and it accurately modelled every one of them. On one occasion, it predicted a weather event that indicated a very high probability of critical peak demand on the electricity system later that evening. As we were still in the early stages of a demand response pilot, we included a step in the process where a very experienced senior engineer would review the recommendations. He said the recommendation was wrong and that there would not be a system peak at the time the model predicted. As you may well know, calling a demand response event is expensive. You have to mobilise your internal team, engage customers, and then pay incentives based on the energy that has been conserved or shifted. You don't want to run an event if you don't have to. So, we followed the advice of the senior engineer and did not call the event. That evening saw the highest demand on our system that year. The data was right.

When I talk about data, I talk about the raw data that you apply algorithms to in order to identify patterns or specific issues. For example, patterns in power quality within a meter can detect energy theft, even when the other measures – such as tamper detection systems – have been bypassed. They can help you determine the shape of a customer's energy consumption, so you know whether they are a good candidate to approach to help reduce high demand on the system at a certain time of day.

There is, of course, a risk with data. And that is the filters and assumptions that are being applied to it before it gets to the decision-maker. An obvious example is when writing a business case. How many times have you seen a business case succeed or fail, or a certain option be selected, even when your gut feel tells you a different outcome should have occurred? Dig deep into the assumptions, and you often see the raw data has been passed through a filter that sways the outcome a certain way. This is not to say anything untoward has happened. This is to say that people, with the best information they have available to them at a particular time, will apply their assumptions to raw data and an outcome is created. These assumptions are often based on an individual's or team's own bias, rather than what the data is really telling them.

I am not suggesting we replace the experience and expertise of our engineers. But we are entering a time of change. A time when our senior experts need to be brought along on the journey, so they are comfortable challenging their own opinion based on real data. If they do not believe the data, encourage them to challenge it to make sure both the data and the assumptions applied are accurate. Once they trust the data and assumptions being applied, you will have their buy-in, and more timely and accurate decisions can be made.

This area cannot be overlooked. I have seen countless businesses make suboptimal decisions, despite having the best intentions.

When we looked back over the data, it was clear the decision was wrong. Unfortunately, the decision-makers and their advisers either did not know the data was available, did not know how to turn that data into useful insights, or simply did not want to use the insights for whatever reason.

In developing the ENERGY framework, I explored over 100 services that could be delivered to help improve customers' lifestyles and give them greater choice. These services also help utilities reduce their operational costs, improve the safety and reliability of supply, and create new partnership opportunities. The vast majority relied on taking the raw energy data from the meters, then applying a level of data analysis to provide the insights required to deliver the service. For example, when you are only recording a customer's energy consumption once every two months, you have no idea when they are using that energy throughout that two-month period. With smart meters, data is captured more frequently, such as every thirty minutes. With this level of data, you can identify patterns to show when energy is used throughout the week. These patterns can be used to offer a range of services to customers. One example is an unusual bill alert service. When a customer receives a high energy bill it is often an upsetting experience, and may prompt them to call the utility because they assume they have been incorrectly billed. In addition to the upset this causes the customer, it costs the utility money to handle that call and manage the enquiry. With an unusual bill alert, the system can identify that energy usage for a specific period, such as one week, has significantly increased compared to previous weeks. Using this information, a utility can immediately notify the customer that they have seen a sudden increase in their energy usage, which will result in higher bills. The utility can ask whether the customer has recently purchased new appliances in the home, whether they have friends or family staying with them, and so on. This raises the customer's awareness of any potential changes in their consumption behaviour that may lead to an increase in their energy usage, and shows that the utility has not done anything wrong (like billing them incorrectly). Without applying analytics to the energy data, such services will not be possible.

That brings us to the end of Chapter 3. By now, you should have an idea of some of the changes that may need to occur within your company. We'll expand on that in Chapter 4, where I reveal four often-overlooked industry insights. But first, here's a list of the key points discussed in Chapter 3:

- You need to focus on services over technologies. Think about the services you want to deliver and why, rather than how you will deliver them and the technologies required.

- If you focus too heavily on the technical aspect of service delivery, this will limit the value you can create, as it immediately places a constraint over what is possible. In contrast, by focusing on the services you want to deliver, and why you want to deliver them, your priority is always on your customers rather than your capabilities.

- With the data that is becoming available to us through smart meters and other sensors, we no longer have any excuse for failing to measure the performance of our operations, or our customers' consumption behaviour. We can increase our knowledge through the availability of energy data.

- For many utilities, this requires a shift in mindset and business approach. Traditionally, most business decisions relied on the gut feel of very experienced senior engineers, where data is filtered to support their view. However, utilities are now shifting to a culture that relies more on the insights derived from data, with senior engineers being involved in the process to make sure the assumptions and filters being applied to the analytical models are appropriate.

Chapter 4:
Four key principles to fast-track your success

Before I reveal my six-step ENERGY framework to you, I'd like to highlight the four principles that I believe will accelerate your path to becoming a successful digital utility.

In our bid to increase customer lifetime value, we often tend to dream up elaborate strategies, which typically require huge resources in terms of funding, people, time, and so on. Before we explore such elaborate strategies, there are steps you should take to put solid foundations in place. These foundations will put your organisation in good stead to succeed over the long term. In this chapter, I reveal four key principles that have the potential to fast-track your success.

Ignoring these principles may not mean you will fail in your goal to become a digital utility delivering value to your customers. But it does mean you are likely to hit a lot of unnecessary problems along the way. In Principle 1, for example, I talk about the need to invest in smart meters. If you look at those utilities more advanced in their journey to becoming a digital utility, you will notice they have invested in smart meters. Look at ComEd in Chicago, AGL Energy in Australia, CLP Power in Hong Kong. These and many more are seen as leaders in their fields, and all of them are rolling out smart meters.

In Principle 2, I talk about starting with the basics. If you look at a wide range of maturity models in other disciplines, such as software development, there are steps to take you from the basics through to optimised. It is the same here – there is no fast path to optimising your use of energy data; you must get the basics right first, or you will be building on shaky foundations.

In Principle 3, I talk about the need to think and operate like a start-up within your organisation. In 2010 I was working for an organisation with dozens of smart-grid pilot programs under way, all of which were being run from within the main business units. They were not coordinated, did not have a clear goal, and were unable to challenge the status quo as they reported to the very business unit they were meant to be disrupting. As soon as we created a separate group within the organisation that had the mandate to act like a start-up, we started to see real wins.

Finally, in Principle 4, I talk about making data available to third parties. If you look at the trends, governments around the world are determining that consumption data is the property of the consumer. Once that policy decision is made, we see a journey where the utility is expected to make it easier and easier for customers to access their data. Rather than waiting to be told, get on the front foot and be at the heart of making this data available. It will build trust through transparency with all your stakeholders, and put you in the driver's seat when working through future regulatory changes. So let's take a look at each principle in a bit more detail.

Principle 1: Invest in smart meters

I often hear people challenging the value of smart meters, often claiming the investment cannot be justified. Smart meters are at the heart of a digital utility. Being digital means leveraging digitised data to gain insights into the behaviour of your customers and the performance of your business, so that appropriate action can be taken.

You cannot be a digital utility without smart meters, or, at the very least, remotely read electric meters. This is the one device that sits on every point on your network that consumes energy, and provides you with incredible granularity into the behaviour of your customers and the performance of your network. Approving a full-scale rollout of smart meters is difficult on many levels. Even with a positive business case, there are political and community hurdles. For example, in Victoria, Australia, the state government mandated the rollout of smart meters without effectively engaging customers and the community. As a result, the residents and businesses of Victoria saw their electricity prices increase to cover the costs of the new technology without understanding its value for them. The public backlash was significant and, as a result, no other state government, or the federal government, is supporting a mandated rollout of smart meters in Australia. As a utility, you need to find a way to start the journey. This may be to roll out smart meters to a small part of your customer base where there is an obvious direct benefit. You may want to simply make the decision that all new and replacement meters are to be smart.

Competitors are emerging that are looking to bypass your energy meter to collect consumption data in other ways. That data will not be available to you as the electric utility. This means your customers will be installing devices and buying services from third parties that help them change the way they consume electricity.

Whatever path you need to take to move forward with smart meters, take it. Sitting back and not making a decision – because you have not been instructed by the regulator, or because you cannot justify the rollout – will only hurt you in the long run.

If you haven't started your smart meter journey to collect energy data, I'll show you how to go about doing this in the chapters that follow, using my six-step ENERGY framework.

Principle 2: Start with the basics

The journey to becoming a digital utility – one that is performing to a level where there is a measurable increase in the lifetime value to your customers – takes time. Foundational investments need to be made and core services put in place. I have written a series of blog posts about the smart metering maturity model. (You'll find those blog posts at www.chapel-group.com.) Basically, they talk about the multi-year journey to fully optimise your operations based on energy data. The mistake we often see is an impatience to start delivering some of the more advanced services, but settling for mediocrity with the basic services. You take your eyes off ensuring the basics that were promised are fully delivered. The returns committed to in the business case (more on this in Chapter 8) start to fail, and you lose confidence in the investments you have made.

To use smart meters as an example, a successful approach to smart metering investments should see a focus on first containing costs and getting key services (such as remote meter-reading and meter management operations) working well. You then move on to reducing your costs in other areas, such as eliminating estimate reads and the related customer enquiries, reducing non-technical losses, and introducing new pricing products to customers. The third step has you improving the customer experience, whereby you may offer predictive bill alerts and abnormal consumption alerts. You may also offer the customer the ability to remotely manage their house move. In the fourth stage, you start to look at how you can offer product and service bundles that support consumer adoption of rooftop solar, local battery storage, smart devices in the home, and a move to electric vehicles. Finally, you use the energy data to connect to the consumer's investments in behind-the-meter technologies. In doing so, you're offering services that allow the customer to enjoy a reduction in their bill – without adversely impacting their lifestyle – by letting you alter their energy usage.

You should explore all stages of the maturity model, and I am not suggesting you must master one stage before progressing to the next. What I am suggesting is that, even when moving on to a later stage, you must remain focused on mastery of the earlier stages. Taking your eyes off these earlier stages will see a slow increase in your cost to serve and a drop in your customer service standards. Once this happens, you'll turn your attention to operational performance, and the longer term, more aspirational investments become a lower priority and start to fall away. Confidence is lost in the investments made and the cycle starts again, with you and your team looking out for the next technology that will help you succeed.

Principle 3: Think like a start-up

Start-ups work to a different set of rules from established companies. The successful ones have identified a problem that needs to be resolved. And they are passionate about resolving that problem. They find ways to work around red tape. They do not have to show quarter-by-quarter growth in revenue, or profits. In fact, many of them will not turn a profit for many years. They have no baggage – they get to operate with a blank sheet of paper, with no corporate policies to follow. If something does not work, they try something else.

As electric utilities, we operate at the opposite end of the scale. Every decision – to secure resources to launch a new initiative, to access funds, or to select a solution – must go through endless steps to demonstrate that the return on investment you are proposing will be greater and faster than that of other proposals in other departments that also want to invest in an opportunity.

The controls we have in place are important, and serve a purpose when making investments that will be applied against the core business. When exploring future opportunities and investing in activities with an uncertain outcome – where the plan is to test and learn – we need to level the playing field with start-ups. We need to recognise that there will be course corrections, and that the path we took on day one will look very different from the service we eventually go live with. We need to set up teams that operate outside lines of business, so they are free to challenge the status quo and are not expected to meet their performance objectives. Ultimately, we need to create our own start-ups within our own organisations, and give them the freedom they need to challenge our core business.

While continuous improvement is most likely a constant in your organisation, when I say you need to think like a start-up, I mean in relation to innovation that will allow you to deliver a step change (a significant change in policy or attitude, especially one that results in an improvement or increase) in a timely manner. Once you have introduced a step change in a certain area of your business, it will then need to be bedded down and, once again, subject to continuous improvement. But you need that step change first. And to do that, you need to think like a start-up.

Until recently, many of your improvement initiatives will have been about reducing cost to serve. As utilities, we are all about repeatability, reliability and driving out cost. Having a competitive cost to serve remains key, but it does not differentiate you. Consumer expectations are changing fast, along with consumers' access to energy services provided by others.

Exploring new ways to deliver customer value means challenging the way you work today. Justifying investments may require a reduction in available headcount and spend for existing lines of business. Running pilots will mean certain activities do not meet the stringent requirements enforced by lines of business. You will also find that these new services you want to explore cross many lines of business, which means cross-business-unit collaboration (something that, historically, has not come easily for many utilities). Lines of business will always put the 'here and now' ahead of the future, as they should. So, my strong recommendation is, as you design your future digital utility – and you come to running pilots, creating business cases, and so on – form a team outside the core lines of business. You need that team to operate without the natural conflicts and interests of the traditional lines of business.

As I said earlier, this new team needs to be encouraged to think like a start-up. But what exactly does that mean? When I have done this previously, I tend to put in place the following principles.

Start-up principle 1: Ditch the corporate mindset

Whenever faced with a challenge, ask yourself: What would a start-up do? Don't force this new team to work within the constraints of the mainstream business. As an example, let's look at enterprise architects, who play key roles within an organisation. Much like a city planner, they are tasked with making sure everyone can access common services to avoid duplication of investment and unnecessary cost. This results in the creation of policies and standards that everyone must follow. This often means new initiatives need to purchase technologies that comply with these standards, as well as fund the integration into existing systems to leverage services that already exist. However, this can hamper innovation. The members of this team need a degree of freedom. Don't force them to use the same back-office applications, to integrate into the mainstream systems, and so on. Let them go it alone, so to speak. If the pilot is showing signs of success, then you need to work with colleagues – such as the enterprise architects – to determine if and when this solution should integrate with corporate systems.

Start-up principle 2: Forget the ROI

This is a bold statement. What I mean here is: Think of start-ups that have an idea how to solve a problem. They will find creative ways to become a success. They run lean, and they leverage what they can. They partner. They are resourceful. What they don't do is sit down and write out a business case with a return on investment that, if unsuccessful, means they stop trying. The single biggest blocker for innovation in most organisations today is that they need to follow the existing corporate practices for investment proposals, and they need to compete against others for funding. Let's say you have a line of business that can demonstrate a positive return on investment (ROI), within the next twelve months, to incrementally reduce cost to serve, up against a new idea where there is no certainty of a return, let alone what that return will be and when it will come through. Which one would you choose? This team's performance certainly needs to be measured, but not using traditional ROI models alone. For example, I like to introduce a measurement similar to that of the company 3M, which expects thirty per cent of a division's revenue to come from new products introduced over the last four years. In the case of a utility, based on my experience I would expect twenty-five per cent of pilot activities to become services offered to customers within four years. This is not an exact science, but it provides the innovation team with enough room to know they can test and learn, and don't always need to get things right. It also gives company executives confidence that they are not funding activities that will never deliver a return to the business.

Start-up principle 3: Disrupt the core

Entities from outside your organisation are always looking at ways to introduce services that will reduce the relationship you have with your customers and, by extension, reduce your revenue. The best way to defend against that is to make those very services available to the market. If you are already offering them, there is less incentive for a competitor to try to do the same.

Below, I've identified five ways you can disrupt the industry from within. I'll discuss each of these ideas in more detail as we progress through the ENERGY framework. This list is merely to get you thinking about the way your business could be operating.

- **Design from the outside in.** Always ask: What would the customer want? We often get caught up in the constraints of how the business currently operates, which means some very promising ideas may never get off the ground; there is too much focus on the day-to-day operations rather than the big picture. Or, we look at new ideas that deliver value to the utility, but have no direct or indirect benefit for the customer. That's why you must always return to this simple question: Is this going to add customer value?

- **Fail fast and safe.** Structures need to be put in place that reward this team for taking risks, getting things wrong and learning. If every future initiative you invest in is a success, then you have not pushed hard enough. The team should be allowed to run pilots. These pilots must have clear success criteria, which is achievable. Applying traditional ROI expectations to innovation initiatives often makes no sense. Instead, the ROI needs to be focused on the potential benefits to the organisation if the pilot is successful and is scaled out to its target customer base.

- **Be secure, open and interoperable.** You need to operate in a mode where others can easily integrate with you. You don't want to use proprietary technologies that prevent you from working with lots of different partners. The easier you are to work with, the lower your cost to partner, allowing you to work with a wider range of partners to co-create solutions.

- **Don't go it alone.** The utility of old tried to do everything themselves. Why wouldn't they? They had a large workforce of very smart people. While you may still have a large workforce of very smart people, the world has changed. There are a range of services – in relation to solar, battery, electric vehicles, the connected home, data analytics, and so on – which is likely to be very new to your organisation. This is where you need to build a strong partner ecosystem.

- **Embrace hypotheses-led decision-making.** None of us have any certainty as to what the future electricity market will look like in the areas we operate in. Energy and communication technologies are changing so fast that the next big thing is always just around the corner, and we have no idea what it is. You can no longer rely on historical performance for future decision-making. You can no longer rely solely on the experience of individuals or your existing decision-making tools. These are all based on looking in the rear-view mirror. Instead, using the lead indicators, knowing what is likely to be possible with emerging technologies, and knowing the expectations and desires of your customers, will allow you to develop a set of hypotheses. You can then set about testing these hypotheses in a structured manner. You implement the ideas that work, and learn from those that don't.

This start-up team will make others in the organisation uncomfortable. It will be challenged regularly by your institution. It will be regularly told, 'This will not work.' For this new team to not just survive but thrive, it needs to be resilient and have strong executive support and governance. More on this in Chapter 10.

Principle 4: Share your data

It was once said to me that the reason utilities are finding it so hard to innovate is because sharing information and collaboration has never been rewarded. Quite the opposite, in fact. Success was based on how much you knew above someone else. It was about solving problems that others couldn't. This also applied at the organisational level; being the go-to company was vital to an organisation's success. That's no longer the case. The utility of the future will fail or succeed based on how much it collaborates with others. The strength of its partnerships. The sharing of information within the community where it operates. This may all sound counterintuitive. Why make information available if it could potentially be used against you? Why make information available so others can provide services and generate revenue that you could have?

The reason is simple. By making energy data available to others, you create a degree of trust through transparency. You place yourself at the heart of the journey we are all on to smart cities, and generate opportunities far beyond what you may lose by making the information available. Imagine partnering with a third party who could independently confirm the customer was receiving an accurate bill, or that they were using the best product you offer. What about exposing data to third parties who provide energy efficiency and conservation (EE&C) services to your customers? If that customer was keen to explore EE&C services, they would have done so with or without your help. This way, you are seen as part of the solution, not part of the problem. Imagine reducing the investments you have to make in your own digital channels, such as web and smartphones, to try to satisfy the needs of all your customers. Instead, you deliver the basic services to all your customers, and allow third parties to deliver more specific services. This reduces your costs while satisfying all your customers' needs, and creates partnerships instead of competitors.

Now, imagine taking this a step further, where you are to become a vital data services provider within your community. Think of yourself as an Airbnb or Uber type service for energy. You have the core energy data, you have energy consumers wanting to purchase energy solutions, and you have energy service providers wanting to access your customer base. This opens up any number of new future revenue opportunities.

Earlier I talked about becoming a competitive monopoly, offering services or 'secrets' nobody else does. Understandably, you may be wondering: How can you give away all your data and have secrets at the same time?

I feel very strongly about this, as I believe utilities that refuse to share data will be worse off in the long run as it will fail to build trust with the community and energy consumers.

At the heart of any successful business is a consumer who trusts what that business stands for and what it delivers. Unfortunately, there is a growing mistrust of utilities. This is partly because people do not understand that the regulatory framework a utility works within ultimately drives the investment decisions that determine which services a consumer does, and does not, receive – and at what price. So, a utility must build trust. There is no better way to build trust than by being transparent.

You are, or I hope you will soon be, collecting vast amounts of consumption data on your customers. This is your *customers'* data. Not making it available to them is analogous to a bank not letting you see the transaction details on your bank statement. Banks have gone from sending their customers quarterly statements to enabling customers to view transactions as they occur. As a bank customer, you can export your data to third-party service providers, such as budgeting specialists, to help you better manage your money.

Your utility needs to do the same with energy data. So, what do I mean by 'share your data'?

First, the consumer should have timely access to their energy consumption via your various digital channels. You should be gleaning insights from this data and providing various value-add services so customers can optimise their consumption without compromising their lifestyle. You need to take this further. You need to make it possible for the customer to authorise third parties to access that data in a standard format. This will allow third parties to offer services to the customer that you have chosen not to, or which the customer prefers over your service offering (remember, you want to be part of the solution, not part of the problem).

The best example of this is the Green Button Initiative in the US. (The Green Button Initiative is an industry-led effort to provide utility customers with easy and secure access to their energy usage information.) I say this is the best example as it is the largest program of its type in the world. Through the Green Button Initiative, sixty million households and businesses in the US are to access their energy data and approve a third party to access it as well.

The customer should be able to easily endorse a third party and, from then onwards, the data should be made available as soon as the utility has processed it. In most cases, this is daily. This scares a lot of utilities. This now means third parties can offer product evaluation services to make sure the customer is on the best possible rate. As mentioned earlier, they can offer customers bill validation services to make sure you are billing them correctly. They may offer energy conservation services, which will reduce your revenue. To all of those risks, I say bring it on. Your customers have a right to this information, and if you are delivering a great service, these value-add services will just strengthen the relationship they have with you. For energy conservation, you need to work with your regulator to be incentivised to encourage more of this. In the meantime, the number of people actively trying to conserve energy is so low that the trust this builds – and the future opportunities it creates – well outstrips any short-term loss of revenue through conservation.

As I mentioned earlier, it also opens up exciting opportunities to create a partner ecosystem. There will be many organisations, large and small, keen to develop applications that leverage energy data captured from smart meters. By helping develop this ecosystem, you become a core component of it and, over time, may be able to monetise this by providing value-add services to those partners so they can further improve their offerings. As an example, you may be able to partner with someone who can validate the bills you are sending to your customers. You probably do this in-house, but what if a third party can provide this service more accurately and at a lower cost? More importantly, how much would your reputation improve if you were able to tell your customers that their bill is validated by an independent third party before being sent to them?

Another approach is to ensure the data is anonymous and make it available via open data channels. In countries such as the UK, there are organisations like the Open Data Institute, which is dedicated to bringing together governments, businesses and communities to access data in order to address particular challenges. By becoming part of this open data community, you can make large, anonymised datasets of energy data available. These datasets, used alongside other information such as weather, emissions data, and so on, can help governments and businesses alike solve specific problems or open up opportunities yet to be identified. The value to the utility is to develop positive relationships with government departments and organisations you may not usually engage with. Having highly influential organisations supporting your plans to implement sensor technologies, such as smart meters – and, in some cases, assisting with their funding – can help remove barriers to entry. Providing these datasets is key to the move to smart cities where applications will rely on access to open data.

The final approach is making data openly available to systems vendors that you partner with. For example, system error messages coming from the smart meters of multiple utilities can be used by the smart metering vendor to get an early line of sight on potential quality issues, and address them before they impact each utility. Smart meters generate a wide range of information about the performance of the meter and the network. There is so much information being generated that it often gets ignored by utilities, which are often focused on other priorities, such as reading the energy consumption recorded in a meter.

Start simple and don't reinvent the wheel. Leverage standard formats already adopted (such as Green Button) that offer partnership programs. If you know you have poor-quality data that leads to inaccurate billing, fix this first. Or partner with a third party who can use this data to perform the analysis on your behalf. Then you can fix your issues. Making energy data available to the consumer, the community and the government will only provide a positive return if the data is timely and accurate.

Where you encounter strong resistance to do this within your organisation, try to understand why. Usually the concern is due to an underlying issue, such as poor-quality data, which, as a utility, you must fix – whether or not you decide to share your energy data.

Ultimately, this is where things are headed. Australia and the UK have rules that support this, and the US has the aforementioned Green Button Initiative.

If you want to create a foundation of trust with your customer, be transparent. The best way to be transparent with your customer is to open up access to their energy data. But don't waste time. With advancements in behind-the-meter technologies, your customers will soon have access to this data anyway, and then you have lost a key opportunity. Take a leadership position now, while you have the chance.

This brings us to the end of Chapter 4. By now, you should have a clear understanding of the four key principles that have the potential to fast-track your success, and how you can start to apply them in your business. Here's a list of the key points discussed in Chapter 4:

- In our bid to increase customer lifetime value, we often tend to dream up elaborate strategies, but there are also some simpler approaches you can adopt, including four key principles.
- Being a digital utility means leveraging digitised data to access insights into the behaviour of your customer and the performance of your business. You cannot be a digital utility without smart meters, or, at the very least, remotely read electric meters.
- There is often an impatience to start delivering some of the more advanced services while settling for mediocrity with the

basic services. However, you must remain focused on mastery of the earlier stages. Taking your eyes off these earlier stages will see your cost to serve slowly increase and a drop in your customer service standards.

- In order to survive and prosper in this increasingly competitive market, you need to think like a start-up. Start-up principles include ditching the corporate mindset, replacing ROI with some other performance metric, and disrupting the industry from within.

- The future utility will fail or succeed based on how much it collaborates with others. By making energy data available to others – namely consumers and third parties – you create a degree of trust through transparency, and generate opportunities far beyond what you may lose by making the information available.

PART TWO:
THE ENERGY FRAMEWORK

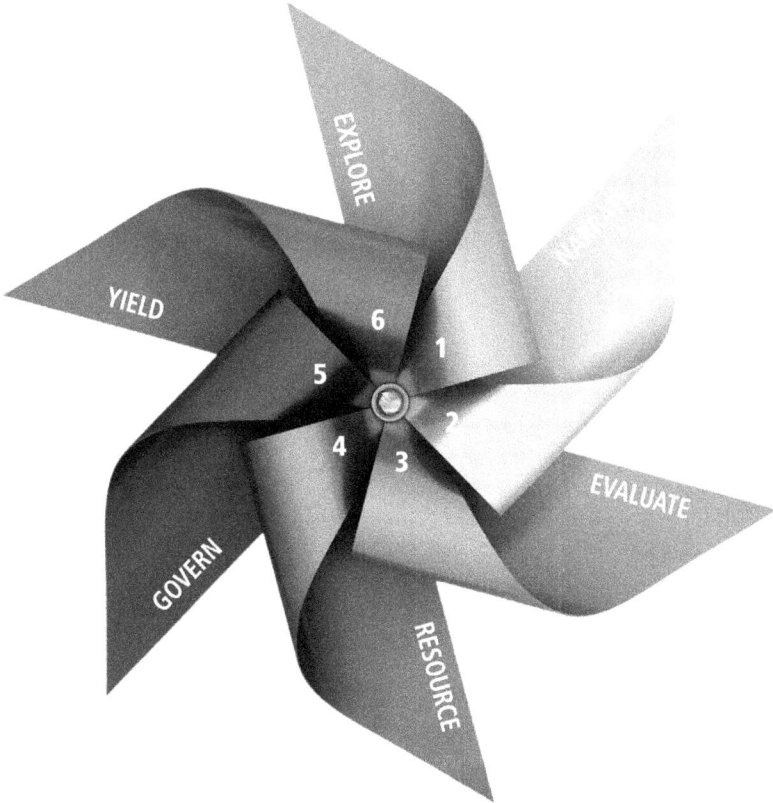

EXPLORE

YIELD

6

1

5

2

4

3

EVALUATE

GOVERN

RESOURCE

Chapter 5:
Introducing the ENERGY framework

To help navigate the coming years of uncertainty, you don't just need a plan that is flexible. You need to collaborate with your stakeholders and bring them on the journey with you. You need to have people on your team staying abreast of the latest advancements in technology, and thinking about how those advancements could apply to your company. You need to have a partner ecosystem that will help you deliver the outcomes you need. You need to think like a start-up, by continuously testing, learning and course-correcting. To help you achieve all of this, I have developed the six-step ENERGY framework: Explore, Narrate, Evaluate, Resource, Govern and Yield.

I came up with this framework to help me in my role as the head of smart grid at one of Asia's most respected electric utilities. In December 2011, I was asked to head a newly formed business unit called Smart Grid Program. Its objective was to determine the costs, benefits and challenges of introducing smart energy technologies into Hong Kong. This included smart metering, demand response, microgrids, rooftop solar, local battery storage, connected homes, electric vehicles, and so on. Reporting directly to the Chief Operating Officer I wasn't tied to any other business units or short-term goals, and could instead focus on the future. I quickly realised that while it was important to understand the technology, this was only a small component. Understanding and managing internal and external stakeholders was critical. Being an architect from a previous life, I did the only thing I knew how to do – I started to create a framework that I could use behind the scenes. A structured approach allowed me to get clear on the end goal, and work back from that to understand all the components that had to fall into place. It was this framework that was the genesis for what has since become the ENERGY framework.

An overview of the 6-step ENERGY framework

The ENERGY framework takes you through six steps to help you leverage energy data to increase customer value and deliver business growth. It helps you develop and execute a roadmap that has the support of all your key stakeholders.

Without people knowing, I applied my framework to over twenty programs that included automated demand response, electric vehicle charging infrastructure, behaviour demand response, smart metering – the list goes on. With each initiative and each lesson learned, I would update my framework. Here's a brief overview of how it looks today.

Step 1: Explore

Before you can introduce a new service, you need to identify your key internal and external stakeholders. Understand what they expect from you and how you are perceived. You need to inform them of what's possible with energy data, and understand what products and services they value, and why.

Step 2: Narrate

You need to be able to tell your stakeholders why you are embarking on this journey. You need to describe what it is you are trying to achieve. Be clear on what's in it for each stakeholder. What are your goals, and how will you know when you've achieved them?

Step 3: Evaluate

You know the outcomes the business is looking for and the expectations of your stakeholders. You now need to translate these expectations into a set of deliverables. These deliverables are not a set of technologies; they are a set of services that are designed to increase the value to your customers. You need to define what those services are. You need to have a view of where you are today with those services. You then need to develop a roadmap that closes the gap between where you are today and where you need to be to introduce these services.

Step 4: Resource

You need money and partners to do all of this. That means justifying your proposed spend and getting the support you need. You will be looking to explore new paths that have no certainty of return. In other areas, there will be a return on investment, but key stakeholders may not support you. Where you can justify investments and secure stakeholder support, you can move ahead. Where you can't justify the investment or lock in support, you may need to invest seed money and test things out. Either way, you need to secure resources. Once justified, you need to find partners who can help you deliver the services.

Step 5: Govern

There will be lots of stakeholders, all with different views as to how they define success, in addition to many different technologies and partners. For this reason, you need to ensure you have set up the most effective governance structure possible to give your company the best chance for success.

Step 6: Yield

It is important that you do not yield to opinion. Instead, monitor performance of the services you are introducing, and make informed decisions based on what the data is telling you. For example, some services you were planning to introduce will need to be put on hold or cancelled altogether, while other services may need to be brought forward.

A word of advice...

The ENERGY framework is a six-step process to help you leverage energy data to deliver customer value. It helps you develop and execute a roadmap that has the support of all your key stakeholders.

However, there are two things to keep in mind as you explore the framework.

If you do not have a clearly defined business strategy, the output from this six-step process can help inform it. If you do have a clearly defined business strategy, then the output from this process must align with it. If there is misalignment, it must be addressed before any of the services are introduced. You must avoid implementing services, no matter how valuable they may appear, if they are not aligned with the future direction of your organisation. It will confuse and frustrate your customers.

Second, I have found that there is a temptation not to spend the time needed to complete steps one through three properly, and instead jump straight to step four. I would strongly recommend against this. Spending the time to build the necessary foundations – including ensuring your stakeholders are on board with what you are planning to deliver, and are actively supporting it – will be critical in later stages as you start to hit road bumps (because you will!).

Now you should have an overview of the six-step ENERGY framework. In the coming chapters, I'll break down each step in detail, starting with Explore. So, without further ado, let's get stuck in.

Chapter 6:
Explore

The first step of the ENERGY framework is Explore.

In this step, you'll learn how to identify the level of influence and interest of your internal and external stakeholders in your journey to becoming a digital utility, and ensure those stakeholders understand what services can be introduced. You'll also discover what services your customers want, and why, and define how you will measure the success of the services to be introduced.

This is the vital first step that sets the foundations for the rest of the ENERGY framework. By completing this step, you will have started the journey of engaging those stakeholders most important to the success of this program. You will get an understanding of their perception of the services you provide today, and the expectations they have of you for the future.

Skipping this step is equivalent to building a house without asking the owners what they expect from you, and also failing to ask the neighbours if they will support what you are planning to build. Without that key support, you'll struggle to complete the project successfully. So, the first thing you need to do is identify your stakeholders.

Know your stakeholders

If you want your utility to succeed, you have to identify who your external and internal stakeholders are, why they are important to you, and then engage them to find out their expectations and perceptions of you. In short, you need to bring them along for the journey. Bringing your stakeholders along for the journey can make or break the success of the services you are looking to introduce. A good example here is with the introduction of new ways to calculate how customers are to be charged for their energy consumption. Historically, the calculation is based on the total energy consumed over a period of time. The introduction of time-based pricing is considered by many economists a fairer way to charge for energy use, as it better represents the costs of generating and delivering the energy to the consumer. Regardless of this, changing the way customers are charged for energy is a sensitive topic. If the community is not effectively engaged, they will push back hard on the utility, stating it will make them pay more for electricity when they most need it. Governments, not wanting to make unpopular decisions, are likely to support the pushback from the community and disallow the introduction of these new ways of charging customers. Understanding your stakeholders and their expectations will help you avoid the project being derailed.

There are two types of stakeholders: Internal and external. Internal stakeholders are entities within a business (employees, managers, the board of directors and investors). External stakeholders are entities not within a business itself, but who care about or are affected by its performance (customers, regulators, investors and suppliers).

So, who are your internal and external stakeholders? It may seem obvious, but it helps to create a list, with one column marked 'Internal' and another column marked 'External'.

To identify your external stakeholders, you should engage those internal stakeholders who have relationships with external stakeholders. In this instance, it is recommended you engage people from departments such as public affairs, account management and senior management. They will help you identify who your external stakeholders are and allow you to answer the following questions about them:

- Do they have a negative or positive view of where you are now, and what you are trying to achieve?
- Do they have a lot of influence, or are heavily impacted by the outcomes of what you are trying to achieve?
- Who in your organisation manages the relationship with them?
- How often will you reassess the health of this relationship?

Once you know who your external stakeholders are, and have completed the above analysis, you can develop a stakeholder management plan. This plan will describe the output from the above analysis. It will then describe who you will engage, when you will engage them, and what messages you will give them.

Examples of external stakeholders include special-interest groups, non-government organisations, chambers of commerce, industry bodies such as telecommunications and transportation, local universities, local government, local community groups, and various media outlets relevant to the energy industry.

In parallel to completing the external stakeholder analysis, you need to work on the internal stakeholder analysis. Working with senior managers, you need to identify the people who would have an interest in this initiative, and what their level of influence would be. As before, once you have completed your assessment, you need to create a stakeholder engagement plan, or, as it's more frequently referred to, a change management plan.

Once you have completed your analysis, you will have a view as to how much influence and interest your stakeholders have over the services you are looking to introduce. However, it's important to note that this is subject to change.

Your stakeholder analysis and the associated engagement plan is a living, breathing document, in the sense that the interest and influence of a stakeholder will change over the course of your journey. As such, you must remain engaged and listening to the feedback you are receiving.

Determine what's possible

Now that you have a good understanding of who your stakeholders are, and their varying levels of influence and interest, you may think it's time to engage them. But first, you need to know what is possible within your business, specifically in relation to energy data. This step is important to ensure you maintain credibility with your external stakeholders. During the consultation stage with your external stakeholders, you want to understand the services they would like to see from you. In most cases, they do not know what they want – they are expecting you to lead them. To do this, your team must have an in-depth understanding of what services can be introduced by a digital utility.

This can be achieved by arranging innovation workshops, where you pull together experts from around the organisation, and invite your technology partners (who are involved in new energy technologies) to participate. The objective of an innovation workshop is simple: To explore what is possible from energy data.

I have run a number of these workshops. I started by removing any constraints people may have in relation to how the organisation works today, the limitations of current technologies, and so on. My team and I achieved this by asking the workshop attendees to imagine a scenario where they could:

- Collect consumption, maximum demand, power quality, and any other key data points at sub-second granularity.

- Either bring the data back from the device that was capturing it whenever you need it, or have the outcome you are looking for delivered by the device itself without having to send all the data somewhere else. In simple terms, have an app on the device that can deliver a specific outcome.

- Contact the device, make changes to what it does, and install new features and fixes. Basically, never have to visit the device unless something physically goes wrong with it.

- Control the device, for example with smart meters, to connect or reconnect power to the premise.

- Have the device alert you when certain events are triggered. For example, smart meters can tell you when they have lost power – an indication that the premise they are monitoring has also lost power.

Setting this as the backdrop for the workshop gave people the permission to think creatively. We then asked the workshop participants to identify real challenges they were facing. We looked at the challenges having the most negative impact on the organisation, and started working through them to see how we could resolve them with access to energy data.

When we ran these workshops, we deliberately divorced ourselves from any known technology. Why? Because all of the scenarios I described previously are possible. They may not have been possible with the technologies or partners we had in place at the time, but we did not want to let this stop us exploring future opportunities.

I found these to be powerful workshops. They freed my colleagues from working within the constraints of what they knew was possible today. It allowed them to focus on their own areas of expertise, to focus on the problems that had to be solved, and explore how those problems could be solved using the possibilities described above.

By the end of each workshop, which can be spread over a few days, we had identified a whole range of services that could be considered part of our developing roadmap. From this, we were able to develop a series of hypotheses, each one describing a service that we believed the customer would want, why they would want it, and why we would want to introduce it.

Once we had identified possible new services, we placed them into one of the following six categories: Lifestyle, choice, operations, insights, partners and enabling services. The categories are important as they help simplify conversations. Trying to explain dozens of services to customers – in fact, to any stakeholder – is difficult. You start to lose people.

Note that each service may deliver value that crosses multiple categories. That's okay. But it is important to communicate the primary value to the consumer, to avoid confusion and maximise appeal.

If a service does not fall into one of the following categories, then you need to question who it's delivering value to, and whether it's really a service you want to introduce. Service categories are described as follows:

1: Lifestyle

These are the services that make a customer's life easier. Remember, the vast majority of people only think about electricity when they have to (moving house, reviewing household budgets, and so on). So, this is all about trying to make people's lives easier. Some examples here are helping the customer move house with just a few taps on their smartphone (yes, this is possible). Another example may be to let them set up a target budget for their energy consumption and, through predictive analytics, send them alerts when they are trending over the budget. You can also provide the customer with hints as to what they can do to stick within their budget. This service means the customer doesn't have to constantly check their consumption and work out how to reduce it. In short, it delivers convenience.

2: Choice

These are the services that directly help the customer reduce their impact on the environment or reduce their energy bill. This can be done by sharing insights into a customer's consumption habits so they can change their consumption behaviour, or by offering financial incentives that may relate to when the customer uses energy, the maximum amount of energy they use, or a combination of both. The solutions will include changes to consumption behaviour through the introduction of behind-the-meter solutions, such as rooftop solar and battery storage, as well as more efficient and more intelligent home appliances and devices.

3: Operations

A large part of the customer's bill covers the cost of the networks needed to deliver the energy, as well as the operational costs to manage the relationship with them. This includes billing, customer service and reading meters. The services in this category can help reduce your cost to serve. This can include reducing non-technical loss, which can occur as a result of energy theft, or incorrect configuration of any part of the metering and billing systems.

In this area, we also look at the safe and reliable supply of electricity, as this is at the heart of every economy. Experiences differ across the world – some countries are still trying to avoid the regular loss of power to large areas, while residents in other countries would not be able to remember the last time they lost power. Services in this category focus on ways of further improving the safety and reliability of supply, such as a smart meter knowing when it has lost power and sending a signal to the utility that informs them of the event. This helps the utility identify the scale and cause of the power outage much more quickly.

4: Insights

Here we look to introduce services that apply advanced analytics to energy data to provide insights that allow improved tracking of key performance metrics. Examples include using energy data to better understand the costs associated with supplying energy to customers; helping calculate customer profitability and customer lifetime value; and helping to understand why customers may be choosing to leave you for another provider. Generating more accurate models, which describe the different types of customers you have, helps you target customers more effectively with certain offers.

Services delivered within this category will not deliver direct value to your customer. Instead, this area focuses on ensuring you and your peers have the right information at your fingertips to make more informed investment decisions. For example, by implementing services that reduce non-technical loss, automate meter reading and eliminate your estimated reads, you should see a large reduction in your cost to serve. If you have implemented these services and you are not seeing a relative drop in cost to serve, then there is an issue that needs investigation.

5: Partners

Here, I'm referring to services that introduce partnership opportunities. Creating a partner network can be quite confronting for many utilities. Historically, a utility does not tend to partner with others, especially other industry verticals. The utility would often enter into business-to-business relationships, referring to them as partnerships, but they were still vendor relationships where the utility was paying a third party to deliver a service to them. An example here is contracting out meter reading services.

What I mean by 'partnership' is to enter into a relationship where both parties are investing resources, and are sharing both the risks and rewards associated with an outcome. This can include working with other critical infrastructure organisations to share the technologies being used to access data from sensors at the edge of the network. For example, the applications and networks used to collect data from an electricity smart meter are the same as those being used for gas and water smart meters. There is no reason why the costs of this technology infrastructure cannot be shared to reduce the overall costs for all organisations.

6: Enabling services

The sixth category is to capture what I call the enabling services. These are services that do not directly deliver value to a customer, but are necessary if you are to introduce services that *do* deliver value. One example is remote meter-reading. You cannot provide customers with certain services – such as predicting their bill, and notifying them when there is unusual activity on their account – unless you are remotely reading their meters.

Many of these services may be outsourced by utilities. However, you need to ensure they are done well. Done poorly, they will cost more money to operate than they should, and prevent you from delivering value to your customers.

Your customers, after all, are your key priority. So, with any service you introduce, you need to get their buy-in. I'll explain how you can do that in the section below. But before I do, there's an online diagnostic tool I'd like you to take a look at.

Where are you today?

You'll find the online diagnostic tool at www.digitalutilityscorecard. com. It's anonymous, it's free, and it only takes about ten minutes to complete. It will provide you with an understanding of the primary services you should consider offering to your customers, and whether you are offering them today. For this reason, the tool excludes questions that relate to enabling services. As described above, enabling services are required to support the delivery of all other service types, and do not by themselves deliver any customer value.

Completing the diagnostic is not essential, but it will help you as you make your way through the ENERGY framework. On completion of the online diagnostic, you will better understand how you are leveraging energy data to deliver services across five of the six categories outlined above.

The purpose of completing the survey now is to get an understanding of the types of services you would be exploring as you progress through this six-step framework. There is no need to take action on what the results are telling you.

Capture your customers' thoughts

Your most important stakeholders are your customers. After all, if you don't have customers, you don't have a business. It's therefore vital to find out what your customers are thinking. One of the ways you can do this is via focus groups, where you ask questions in an interactive group setting so participants are free to talk with other group members. The goal of a focus group is to discover people's perceptions, opinions, beliefs and attitudes towards a product, service, concept, advertisement, idea or packaging.

Let me give you an example of how you can use focus groups to inform key business decisions. My team and I once asked a group of customers whether they would consider purchasing an in-home display, or IHD (an energy monitor that electronically reads information from the user's smart meter to help them manage their electricity use). The IHD was a small device with a small display, which would capture the energy consumed, as recorded by the smart meter, and display it in near real-time. The idea was that consumers would see this information and it would influence the way they use energy.

The feedback varied, but there were many people, across a range of different backgrounds, who said they would rather have the information fed straight to their smartphone.

This feedback was key. We decided against the expense of installing IHDs and instead built a smartphone app. In hindsight, this was the right decision for a whole range of reasons, including the fact that installing IHDs would have added another cost to the program with little to no additional benefit. Had we not engaged our customers, the team – mostly made up of technologists and engineers – may have pushed ahead to test a technology that customers would have rejected.

I am not suggesting customer feedback in focus groups is always right. We often received feedback that, after analysis and discussion, we dismissed. What I am saying is that engagement is key. You need to focus on capturing your customers' thoughts so you can make informed decisions.

Running focus groups may already be standard practice within your organisation. So before you start from scratch, speak to your colleagues to find out if this is the case. You can save a lot of time and effort by tapping into something that is already up and running.

If focus groups are not being run, you can engage a specialist organisation for support, as it's important that the focus groups are both structured and executed well. Alternatively, if you decide to do it yourselves, then think about the following:

- **How many focus groups will you run?** I would typically look at as many groups as there are customer segments. So, one per customer segment. If you have more than eight customer segments, consider grouping them. Running more than eight focus groups gets very time consuming and costly, and is unlikely to reveal any new insights.

- **How many people should be part of each focus group?** There is no hard and fast rule, but each focus group should consist of approximately eight customers. More than this and I find there are members of the group who will dominate discussions, and you lose the value of having everyone contribute.

- **Who should be part of each focus group?** Each focus group should represent a certain aspect of your customer base. This could include retired people who spend most of their time at home, professional couples with no children, families that have at least one parent at home most of the time, and so on. The reason for grouping people together in this way is to identify any patterns emerging from people in similar situations.

- **How long does each focus group last?** I typically expect each focus group to last three to four hours.

- **What questions should you ask?** The purpose of the focus group is to get an idea of whether the attendees understand the types of services you are considering, and whether they support their introduction. As you proceed through the ENERGY framework, you are potentially going to explore 100-plus services. There is no way you can cover all of these in the focus groups you run. I usually select services that, if introduced, may not be positively received by customers, or may need the customers' involvement to be successful. This would include services that change the way you calculate customers' energy use for their bills, such as introducing demand- or time-based tariffs, and any service that relates to demand response, where I am asking the customer to significantly change their consumption behaviour for a few hours to help conserve power.

- **What should you do with the information?** Focus groups are designed to inform your thinking. You do not have to implement everything these customers tell you. They are, after all, the opinions of only a few people.

What I recommend is for you to sort the responses into observations, such as: 'Most people did not understand why you would charge more for electricity when they needed it the most.' This becomes a very important input with regard to how you will raise awareness and educate customers on this topic in the future. In all of the focus groups I've been involved in, we always received valuable feedback.

Define how you will measure success

At this point, you have an understanding of what is possible with energy data, and have formed a view of the services you may want to introduce. You have started to engage consumers, most likely in the form of focus groups, and are gaining feedback on the services you're looking to introduce.

It's now time to start thinking about how you will measure success. The reason this is so important at this early stage is because you will struggle to secure support from customers and other stakeholders later in this process if you cannot describe what success looks like. You will be surprised how many utilities are not measuring the performance of many of the services that they are already delivering.

There are a series of top-line measurements that are key to utilities, and I call these primary metrics. Not all are applicable – it depends on the regulatory environment you operate in. For example, in a competitive retail market such as Australia, it is important to track the costs associated with both losing a customer to a competitor, and winning a customer from a competitor. These performance metrics do not apply to a regulated utility, which provides services to customers based on where they live, as opposed to the customer choosing who to receive a service from.

At a minimum, the primary metrics I would recommend you focus on are:

- Cost to serve.

- Cost to acquire a new customer, where applicable.

- Cost to retain an existing customer, where applicable.

- Customer profitability.

- Customer lifetime value.

- Net promoter score, which measures how likely someone is to recommend your services. This is a good way to track customer loyalty.

- Customer satisfaction score, which is a basic measure to track whether customers are happy with the service you are providing.

- Supply reliability using SAIDI (System Average Interruption Duration Index) and SAIFI (System Average Interruption Frequency Index) figures. SAIDI is the average outage duration for each customer served, while SAIFI is the average number of interruptions that a customer would experience.

- Enquiries and complaints, where you track the number of enquiries and complaints as a percentage against your customer base or a particular section of your customers.

When you look at the value of introducing a service, you will determine the benefit of introducing that service. For example, demand response may result in you deferring investments in infrastructure and therefore reducing your capital expenditure. I classify this metric as a secondary metric. The secondary metric is important to be able to track the performance of a service. However, it is of little value to the customer. You need to tie each service back to one of the primary metrics above. In this example, demand response would reduce your cost to serve – a primary metric. For this reason, it is important to know how the services you will introduce will improve these metrics.

In all cases, you should be able to tie services to a primary metric. For example, in the area of cost to serve, you can look at minimising consumption on accounts that have been marked inactive. You can also reduce the costs of reading a meter or producing a bill, and you can eliminate estimated reads, which result in unnecessary customer enquiries and complaints.

In many cases, you may find that you are not recording secondary metrics, or at least not in a way that allows you to accurately measure the performance of a new service. The simple rule of thumb for deciding whether a new service should be introduced is if you can show how it improves one of the primary metrics described above. If you cannot show how the introduction of a new service, or the improvement of an existing service, will contribute to primary metrics such as a reduced cost to serve or an increased net promoter score, then you should be questioning why are you focused on it. For example, not many utilities have a good grasp on customer profitability. That is because they don't fully understand the cost to serve individual customers. For instance, let's say customer A generates more revenue than customer B, but customer A also calls the utility a couple of times a month and complains a lot about their bill. The cost associated with managing these complaints means the profitability of customer A is actually less than customer B. To drive up the profitability of customer A, you need to identify what the underlying issues are and address them. This will stop the customer calling in so much, which means less time and money spent managing complaints, and, as a result, a more profitable customer.

Your organisation is likely to have a standard set of primary metrics in place. This is your opportunity to revisit these with your steering committee (more on this in Chapter 10) and agree which ones will be used, and possibly introduce some more. Once your primary metrics have been agreed on with your steering committee, you can focus on making sure every service you are looking to introduce has a secondary metric in place, so you can track and improve its performance.

Once your primary and secondary metrics are in place, you have baselined your current performance. As you look to introduce a new service, you should be able to describe how this baseline is improved. This will help you secure both stakeholder support and funding for its introduction.

That brings us to the end of Chapter 6, and the end of Step 1 in the ENERGY framework. As I stated earlier, I urge you not to skip over this step. The temptation is to think you know who your stakeholders are and what they want. Even if you do, you must perform this step to include them in the journey and get their support. If you skip this section, you are likely to invest in services that fail, or *not* invest in services that would have been a huge success. This step does not need to take long. It can typically be done within a couple of months, or even weeks (if the right internal and external stakeholders are available to attend meetings and workshops to provide you with the necessary input). Investment in this step will pay significant dividends later.

Before we move on, here's a list of the key points we discussed in Chapter 6:

- Identify your key stakeholders, and understand their perceptions and expectations of your organisation.

- Complete stakeholder analysis to understand the levels of interest and influence of each stakeholder, relative to your proposed program of works.

- Develop an engagement plan for each of your stakeholders.

- Run innovation workshops with senior staff and key partners, so they have a broader understanding of what is possible with energy data.

- Run focus groups with customers to gain initial feedback on potential new services.

- Determine a set of primary and secondary metrics that will be used to measure whether the investments you will be making increase lifetime customer value.

Chapter 7:
Narrate

Your journey to becoming a competitive monopoly – whose services customers seek out, even when they are available elsewhere – must tell a story. In many cases, your utility faces trust issues with the customer, who does not understand why you are investing in certain services, or how those services will directly benefit them. This is why communication is key. But before you communicate with your customers about any new services, you need to gain the support of several major internal stakeholders (senior executives, the board and investors), plus key external partners. Otherwise, there won't be any services to speak of.

In order to gain this support, you must be able to present a compelling narrative. You need to be able to explain what services you want to deliver to your customers, why you want to deliver them, and the resources required to get there. This step is all about winning the hearts and minds of your stakeholders. And it all starts with developing your set of hypotheses.

Develop a set of hypotheses

The *Oxford English Dictionary* describes a hypothesis as: 'A supposition or proposed explanation made on the basis of limited evidence as a starting point for further investigation.' At this stage, you have some information about the services your organisation wants to introduce, and the services your customers want. You need to start building a series of hypotheses for services where you cannot be 100 per cent certain of an outcome.

For example, when you remotely read meters and remove people from the meter reading process, you can calculate the costs and benefits. When you are considering introducing a service that requires a customer to change their consumption behaviour, you have very limited information to know if this service will be welcomed by your customers. For those services, you need to develop a set of hypotheses that can be tested. For example, a set of hypotheses may include the view that:

- Customers will reduce their energy consumption if they are presented with timely and meaningful information, such as alerts that tell them their consumption is higher than usual.

- Customers will reduce their consumption during times of high power demand if they are given adequate notice and sufficient financial incentives.

- Car dealerships will promote your electric vehicle tariffs, as it will help them sell more cars.

In order to gain the trust and support of these stakeholders, you need to come up with an initial set of hypotheses. You need to use these hypotheses to inform what services your organisation wants to deliver, why you want to deliver them, and when.

This usually takes the form of a digital utility roadmap. The road-map shows time from left to right. You would create a section in the roadmap for each of the areas introduced earlier (choice, insights, lifestyle, operations, partners, and enabling services). You would place each service on the roadmap to show when you believe it should, and could, be introduced. If you are introducing it as a pilot to test and see if it works, of if you are planning on introducing it into your mainstream business, I recommend you colour-code the roadmap to show if the service first needs to have secondary metrics created so you can create a baseline. I would suggest setting a timeframe of no more than three years. The environment we operate in is changing so fast that planning anything further out than three years is unlikely to offer any value. New technologies, new competitors, changes to customer expectations and changes to regulatory rules within that time are likely to make any plans beyond three years obsolete.

To develop the set of hypotheses and the digital utility roadmap, you will need to run a series of workshops. Those workshops should not contain any more than twenty people. More than that, and it becomes difficult to facilitate and ensure everyone's views are heard. There should be a workshop for each of the six main areas of choice, insights, lifestyle, operations, partners, and enabling services. You should invite subject matter experts and key decision-makers to the workshops, relevant to their areas of expertise and responsibility.

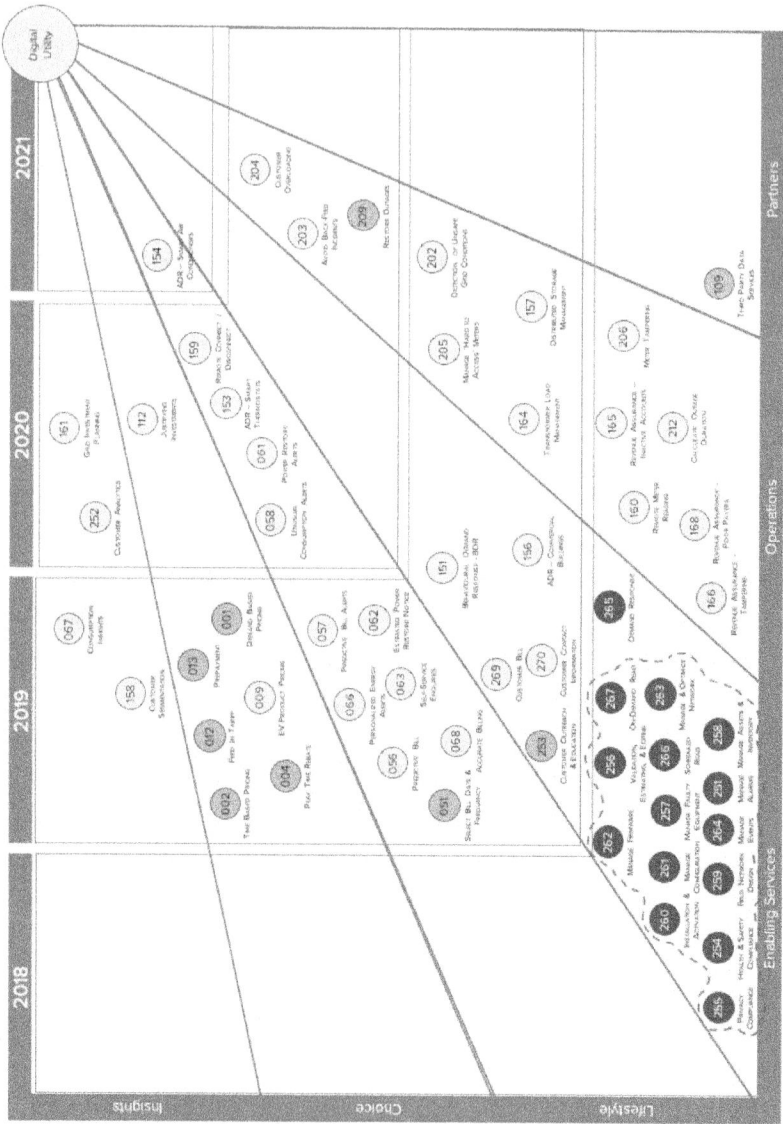

Digital utility roadmap

Once you've developed this initial set of hypotheses and your draft digital utility roadmap, you can start to share it with your aforementioned stakeholders. It's important to remember that you are at the embryonic stages of developing your strategy, so a lot will change. That's why it's so important to get honest feedback from multiple stakeholders.

Within your stakeholder engagement plan developed earlier, you will have identified representatives that your organisation can speak to. Your team needs to share the set of hypotheses and draft digital utility roadmap with these stakeholder representatives. You need to ensure they understand why you are looking to introduce these services. Check they understand the services you are introducing, and are clear on the value these services deliver. You want to ensure the individuals or organisations they represent would support the introduction of such a service, and get feedback on how best to communicate the introduction of these services to that stakeholder group. Where the representative shows concerns, these must not be challenged by your organisation. Instead, they must be recorded and brought back for analysis. At the end of this exercise, you must update your stakeholder engagement plan and determine, for each stakeholder, how and when you plan to start communicating the introduction of each service. This is an iterative process. As you refine your hypotheses and the digital utility roadmap, you will need to go back and update the representatives of your stakeholder groups to maintain an accurate understanding of their perceptions and expectations.

Determine your starting position with the four Ps

Now that you have a view of where you want to get to, you need to perform a current state analysis. In simpler terms, you need to understand your starting position. To help you do that, I have created the four Ps model, adapted from a range of other models I have been exposed to over the years. Whether you are looking at the current or target state of a service, this approach means everyone is on the same page with regard to how that service is placed across four important dimensions. Each of these dimensions needs to be addressed if you are to successfully introduce a service. For example, if you move forward without understanding the policy implications, you may not be able to introduce a service, no matter how much value you believe it will deliver to your customers.

The four Ps stand for policy, people, process and platform.

Policy

Policy can refer to a legal requirement set out by an external entity such as the regulator, telecommunication standards, privacy standards, and so on. It may also be an internal policy your organisation has introduced, such as information security or health and safety. In my experience, policies don't necessarily cost much to change, but changing them does tend to take a long time.

Policies can create barriers for innovation. I have often been in workshops where people have said, 'We can't do X, as we are not allowed to.' When I ask whether they think X is the right answer, assuming they were allowed to do it, often the answer is yes. I am not suggesting all policies can be changed, but they are developed based on what made sense at the time. Policies can become out-dated and do need to be challenged.

One particular example that always comes to mind is the need for an electricity meter to have a display so people can read the consumption data. In a world where the data of smart meters is read remotely, having a display seems unnecessary. You will come up against other equally archaic policies, both internal and external, that will be limiting the creativity of your experts. So, wherever you can, look at your policies and challenge them.

People

People refers to all stakeholders, including your employees. Think about the people who will be involved in each service you're looking to introduce, and whether they will be able to support the rollout of the new services in their current state. For example, are the operational support staff fully trained? Has your organisation created and disseminated standard responses to answer any questions about the service? Are your highly influential stakeholders aware and supportive of the introduction of this service? Are your partners ready to support the service and do they fully understand your expectations of service levels? And, perhaps most importantly, is your target market aware this service is being introduced, and have sufficient steps been taken to educate these consumers about the service?

These questions need to be asked to determine how ready you are to introduce the service, or, where the service has already been introduced, where there may be gaps that need to be closed to ensure the customer's experience of this service is as you envisaged. I recall a situation where we were introducing a pilot program to a set of customers in a certain location. We had taken all the necessary measures we could think of to ensure these customers had been sufficiently engaged, and we were prepared for the questions they may ask. What caught us by surprise was that we were challenged by other residents in the area. They wanted to know why they were not involved and were quite upset. While you will always face technology challenges when exploring new energy technologies, it is always the people-related challenges that present the greatest risks to our projects.

Process

Process covers any processes and procedural activities that need to be completed, so it is very clear how this service will be delivered from start to finish. For example, meter to bill is a process that involves all the activities involved in recording the energy consumption of a customer, through to using that energy data to bill that customer. When introducing smart meters, many activities within an existing process will change.

The biggest mistake I see people making when it comes to processes is not taking an outside-in view. In other words, they look at the process from their own perspective. The problem with this approach is that you start to see tasks being added that an employee may feel are important, but which makes the experience worse for the user (which, in most cases, is your customer). You must take an outside-in view of your processes. This means constantly asking yourself a series of customer-centric questions:

- What is the experience for the user of this service?
- Does it make sense?
- Have we stripped out all unnecessary steps for them?

A typical example is the process for move-in and move-out services (whereby a utility disconnects and reconnects a customer's power when they move house). When you design the process from the inside out, you look to use the remote disconnect and reconnect feature of a meter. As you start working through all the steps, usually based on how you have done things historically, you end up with a process that still involves a lot of steps and delays for the customer.

By contrast, an outside-in view would think about what the customer wants, rather than the technology required. In this example, the customer most likely wants to open up a smartphone application, tell you the date and time they want to be disconnected at one premise, and the date and time they want to be connected at the next premise. That's it. Of course, there are additional details that need to be obtained – such as asking the customer on the scheduled disconnection date to confirm that all appliances and devices have been turned off – but all of this should be seamless for the customer. When you deliver services where the process has been designed from the outside in, it forces you to challenge the ways you have previously worked.

This approach can also be applied to the first P – policy.

Platform

Platform refers to any required investments in technologies. These technologies can be physical devices in the field, the network, or any of the many back-office applications needed to deliver a service.

Platform does not mean one end-to-end solution from one vendor. The days of buying one solution that delivers everything you need are fast disappearing. These large, monolithic platforms served a purpose when the goal was all about reducing cost to serve. However, today that is just one part of the equation. Speed to market, course correction, and being flexible with the services you offer are all becoming just as important.

Consequently, a good approach to technology architecture is becoming paramount, as the end-to-end solution required to deliver a service is likely to include multiple applications all having to seamlessly work together. In a single process, you may have half-a-dozen or more supporting applications. These applications may all come from different vendors. Some of these applications may be based in your own data centre, where you have a high degree of flexibility to change the functions and features, whereas others may be cloud-based and therefore give you limited opportunity to change how they work. With such a complex mix of applications, it means your data is being stored in many locations, so getting a single view of a customer (to calculate cost of acquisition, cost of retention, lifetime value of the customer, and so on) becomes incredibly difficult unless you have a well-architected solution.

Apply the four Ps to your current state analysis

Taking the set of hypotheses you have developed, you will have a draft digital utility roadmap that lists the services – under each of the six categories – that you want to deliver.

The four Ps model will also help you understand the effort involved in introducing a service, as well as determining when would be best to introduce the service. For example, you may want to introduce a service that allows your customer to remotely manage their own move-in and move-out process. On analysis of the policy, you find a rule in place that states a field engineer must first check someone is at home before power is reconnected. This is a safety measure to ensure the previous tenants have not left equipment, such as the oven, turned on, so when power is restored the oven will not come back on and create a fire hazard. This policy is out of date. You can ask the customer to confirm whether someone is home, or that they have checked all appliances are turned off via a smartphone app or a phone call. Nevertheless, while the policy is out of date, it is still the policy. You will need to take advice from subject matter experts on how long that policy would take to change.

Against each of these services, you need to get the right stakehold-ers together who can rate the service against each of the four Ps. To determine the stakeholders needed, it is best to bring together stakeholders who represent parts of the business that will be im-pacted by the introduction of, or changes to, this service. The execu-tives will know who, from the different business areas, you should engage for each service if you are not sure.

Each P needs criteria assigned to it. For example:

- **Policy:** You can flag that the policies either support the service you want to introduce, need some revisions, or need a complete change in direction.

- **People:** You can identify if internal people have been engaged and trained, and whether external people are engaged and supportive. Or you can flag people as still needing to be engaged, and rate them based on whether that engagement effort will be high or low. For example, a service that requires training of a small team, or a single person, would be low. Training of a department may rate medium, and an entire business unit would be high. I recommend you also create an option to flag that there are stakeholders objecting to the introduction of this service in its proposed form.

- **Process:** You need to identify the effort involved in getting the process ready to introduce a new or improved service. You need to determine if the introduction of the service will mean a change to part of an existing process, many changes to an existing process, or if it completely replaces the existing process and introduces a new one. An example is remote meter-reading. Every aspect of this process changes: from how and when you read the meters, to how and when you load the data into your systems, through to how and when you verify that the data is accurate. This is different from introducing a service to receive notifications when a meter loses power, which can be contained to making changes to a small part of the overall outage management process.

- **Platform**: Here you need to identify which technologies need to be changed or introduced, and rate the effort involved. For example, the service may require changes to a single application that your organisation has the expertise to change. Alternatively, the requirement may mean an existing application will need to be upgraded or replaced.

I have used a set of predefined criteria for many years, but you can apply whatever is relevant to your organisation, so long as the criteria are applied consistently across all services. For example, against each of the four Ps, I determine the estimated cost, the estimated time, the estimated complexity, and the estimated dependencies on other services being introduced. I do this using a standard set of criteria, such as:

- **Cost**: Low cost means less than $100,000, medium is less than $500,000, and high is over $500,000. The actual number you use will depend on the size of your organisation.

- **Time**: Low means it will take less than three months, medium is less than six months, and high is greater than six months.
- **Complexity**: Low means only one team is impacted, medium means less than four teams are impacted, and high is more than four teams are impacted.
- **Dependencies**: Low means there are no dependencies, medium is one to three, and high is more than three.

You can record this information in a table, like the one below, to make it easier to refer back to. You should record your findings per service.

	Policy	People	Process	Platform
Predictive Bill Alerts	Today's policy only supports actual or estimated reads for the purpose of billing the customer. The policy will need to be revised to allow us to 'predict' the customer's future energy use, without it being a legally binding value. Low	The call centre staff will need to be trained to answer questions by customers. Specialist resources need to be trained to answer queries the call centre cannot answer. Customers will need to be educated that this is a forecast and may not be accurate. Medium	A nightly process needs to be introduced that can forecast a customer's energy use for the coming bill period. If the forecast value exceeds a value set by the consumer, an alert needs to be sent to the customer. Medium	The current billing system cannot perform these predictive calculations. A solution is required to perform the calculations and to send notification to the consumer. Our digital channels also need to be able to display this information to the consumer. Medium

At the end of this exercise, you will need to revisit your draft digital utility roadmap. You will find that when you had planned to deliver the services will have changed. You need to reflect this in your draft digital utility roadmap.

Once you have a clear view of the services you want to deliver, and how much work is going to be required to deliver them, it's time to develop your narrative.

Develop your narrative

You do not want to simply tell people what services you will be introducing, and when. This goes back to my earlier statement about winning the hearts and minds of your stakeholders. You need to tell them a story that resonates with them. A story where they can clearly see what is in it for them and why they should support it. By developing a strong narrative now, you'll create the necessary foundations to secure support (from your board, the industry regulator, your customer base, your partners and the broader community) further down the track.

At this point, I find it valuable to engage an expert in storytelling. This should be someone who is not close to your initiative and can provide an objective view. I would liken it to writing a book. While the content comes from the author, the editor will make sure the structure of the story comes together, that the story flows and makes sense, that jargon is removed or explained, and that the points you are trying to make are made well. You need to be clear on what messages you want to get across, such as how these services may support the Energy Trilemma, which we covered back in Chapter 2.

I have experienced a huge difference in stakeholder acceptance of a new service when it has been accompanied by a strong, authentic narrative that has been shared consistently by people across the organisation. For example, I was previously involved in discussions about the value of demand response with an energy regulator. I was explaining the benefits of avoiding infrastructure investments, leading to a long-term reduction in the rates a customer paid for electricity. There was zero interest. A short time later, after trying to understand what was important to the regulators at that time, we re-positioned the narrative to being one around the consumer having greater choice and control to conserve energy and save some money. The problem we were trying to solve did not change, neither did the solution. Instead, we changed the narrative to better align with what was considered an important topic to the regulator, and we started to get the support we needed.

Creating a compelling narrative can be done internally – this requires talking to your stakeholders and understanding their priorities in relation to energy. Build a narrative that addresses their concerns, desires and priorities, and play this back to them to refine it. Your marketing or public affairs departments are often great places to start to find a suitable resource to pull this together. If they are unable to help, they will most likely know third parties who specialise in the art of storytelling, as it's now at the heart of all good marketing campaigns.

That brings us to the end of Chapter 7, and the end of Step 2 in the ENERGY framework. Before we move on, here's a list of the key points discussed in Chapter 7:

- Before you communicate with your customers about your services, you need to gain the support of several major internal stakeholders, plus key external partners. Otherwise, there won't be any services to speak of.

- In order to gain this support, you must be able to present a compelling narrative, which starts with a set of hypotheses.

- Once you've developed a set of hypotheses, you need to perform a current state analysis, using the four Ps model as a guideline.

- The four Ps stand for policy, people, process and platform. You should invite stakeholders to rate each service you're looking to introduce against all four Ps, and update your hypothesis accordingly.

- Once you have a clear view of the services you want to deliver, and how much work is going to be required to deliver them, it's time to develop your narrative. You can either do this yourself or hire an expert.

Chapter 8:
Evaluate

You will tell your story in different ways to different people, but the core message –what you plan to deliver, why, and when – should remain consistent. The focus now is on stress-testing your story and the services you are proposing to introduce. If done well, you will get important feedback that improves the narrative and your roadmap, and secures the support of your stakeholders. If done poorly, or not done at all, you are likely to hit problems later in the program. Either influential stakeholders will try to prevent your program from being a success, or services will fail to capture the hearts and minds of the consumer and fail to deliver the expected benefits.

During this evaluation phase, you need to engage all stakeholders who will be affected in some way. This includes those who are receiving the services, the stakeholders who need to fund and approve the introduction of these services, and the stakeholders who need to deliver these services.

You are seeking very specific feedback, and so you need to meet with the various stakeholder groups (more on that later). This is the final step before big money starts to be spent, so it's vital you seek as much feedback as possible. At this stage, you have not developed business cases, and you have not run tenders and entered into partnerships. You have not presented a business case to the company board and the industry regulator. Most importantly, you have not introduced these services to the mass market, and therefore haven't exposed yourself to negative media coverage, which can have adverse impacts on your company well beyond that of the individual project that created the backlash.

Stress-test your narrative

Once you have a strong narrative, it's time to test it out. The initial feedback will more than likely prompt you to revise the narrative. So, you should seek feedback from a wide range of sources.

Looking back to your stakeholder engagement plan, I would look to re-engage the original focus groups, as well as representatives from:

- Local academia – they will have professors and students studying in your field. They are often keen to be involved so they can validate their thoughts against real data, and cost much less than consultants.

- Chambers of commerce – are interested in promoting the businesses they represent. If they believe the journey you are about to embark on will benefit their members, they will provide support.

- Environmental groups – can be both a strong advocate and adversary. Best case scenario is to get their support. Worse case is it helps you prepare for them challenging your roadmap when it becomes public.

- Consumer groups – similar to environmental groups.

- Property developers and managers – would be interested in supporting your roadmap if this helps them deliver better services to their tenants.

- Product and solution vendors – getting vendors excited about your roadmap can lead to them co-creating with you. This leads to more advanced services coming to market faster at lower prices.

- Local and national government – are often the decision-makers, and at the very least are heavily influential. Ensuring they are supportive is vital to a successful digital utility roadmap.

- Industry bodies – similar to chambers of commerce. If your roadmap is seen as valuable to its members, they will provide you with support.

You want to understand their views, good and bad, on your narrative. I would expect this to take a few iterations with the representatives of your various stakeholder groups. The ideal outcome is for everyone to understand and support the narrative. The reality is that some will not support it. That is okay, but you need to develop a plan for how you manage these stakeholders moving forward. Otherwise, they could become very vocally opposed to what you are trying to achieve, which can cause you problems later.

Secure stakeholder support

Once you have the narrative nailed down, you can circle back to those stakeholder representatives who were strong supporters of the narrative to elicit their help in communicating it to the members of their respective stakeholder groups, and therefore expand the support for your initiative.

I am often surprised how little utilities leverage their stakeholders to build broad support for their initiatives. In my experience, you stand a greater chance of getting support for your narrative if the story is being told to an audience by a person they trust and respect. For example, I would have less credibility selling my story to an environmental group than the head of that environmental group telling the same story to his or her members.

To give you an idea of how important this step is, let me give you an example where a utility looked at the introduction of time- and demand-based rates. As you may know, most residential electricity consumers are billed based on the volume of electricity consumed over a given period – say a month. It would not matter when they consumed energy during that period, nor would it matter whether they placed maximum power demand on the system at any one time. (To explain maximum power demand, think of a split-system air conditioner, which may draw one kilowatt of power. If the customer had four air conditioners and turned them all on at the same time, the maximum power demand of those four units is four kilowatts.)

Historically, consumption-based pricing worked well. There was no real understanding of the impact on the environment, so the more power people needed, the more infrastructure the energy companies built. Over time, it became important to look at influencing the way customers consumed energy, so in came block pricing. With block pricing, the more energy consumed, the more the customer paid. If the customer consumed over a certain threshold within a given period of time, the rest of their consumption would be charged at a higher rate. These plans were introduced as they are very easy to explain to a consumer in relation to energy conservation. And, historically, the electricity meters used to track consumption did not support more sophisticated approaches to calculating how customers should be billed for their energy consumption.

The problem is that the amount of energy consumed is only part of what makes up the costs of delivering energy to a customer. Historically, energy is not stored at large scale. It has to be used the moment it is generated, or it is gone. For an electric utility to ensure it can meet the demand of its consumers, it needs to make sure it can generate and distribute that energy at the moment it is needed. The problem here is that for a few hours a year, that demand might be huge compared to other times of the year, when demand may be a lot less. The electric utility must make sure it has enough power for those few hours, so for the rest of the year that infrastructure continues to be maintained in case it is needed, but goes unused. However, the billions of dollars invested still need to be recouped, and so all customers are charged.

So, as you can see, the historical models for billing consumers have a number of flaws. First, they are not fair. Consumers who are not contributing to the demand on a system that is driving up investments in infrastructure, and therefore the electricity rates, are being charged the same as those who *are* contributing to this increase in investment. Second, they provide no incentives to create a demand profile that improves the efficiency of the system, in turn driving down the investments needed, which would lower the rates passed on to everyone.

So, with that in mind, we were looking to introduce new pricing models that would make it fair to all consumers, maximise the efficiencies of existing infrastructure, and minimise the need for future investments. So, when we started to talk to stakeholders about the need to introduce time- and even demand-based pricing, they understood.

Hopefully, you can see from this example the importance of evaluating your story with your stakeholders. This all comes back down to the issue I raised earlier, and that is the need for us, as an industry, to start taking an outside-in look at designing our services, rather than an inside-out view. Time- and demand-based pricing makes complete sense when you look at it from the electric utility's perspective. However, it makes absolutely no sense, at least initially, to the person who will now be paying a lot more money for doing the same as they have always done. That's why it's so important to liaise with your stakeholders, and gain their support, *before* you spend money on a new service or model. To close out this example, instead of forcing people onto new tariffs, the approach that was taken was to offer customers the choice to move onto these tariffs. This removed resistance to the introduction of these services.

Earlier, I suggested running a series of workshops with the various stakeholder groups. In the section below, I'll reveal how to structure those workshops to ensure you gain the necessary feedback and support, enabling you to properly evaluate each service before investing in it.

Stress-test your services

The services you have selected to invest in will fall into one of three categories:

1. **Create baseline.** This is where you have a service, such as reducing non-technical loss, but where you don't currently have measurements in place to know what your actual non-technical loss is. This is always your first step, so you have a starting point to forecast what improvements you expect to make.

2. **Pilot service.** This is where you run a pilot to test an unknown outcome, such as a change in customer behaviour as a result of offering them a financial reward.

3. **Implement service.** This is where you have a high degree of certainty that you can deliver the service within a defined budget and timeframe, as well as having a high degree of certainty over the benefits that will be realised.

During this phase, it is a good idea to use your focus groups to discuss some of the more controversial services you are looking to introduce, regardless of which of the above categories they fall into. A controversial service is anything where you require your customers to take action. For example, if you are looking to introduce demand-based pricing in the form of a particular new product, then stress-test this product with your focus groups.

Evaluate the results

Once you have feedback from the representatives of your various stakeholder groups, you need to evaluate the results, and decide if and how you may change the services you plan to introduce, and when.

You need to reconvene the same workshops that you originally ran when developing your set of hypotheses and draft digital utility roadmap. Review the feedback as a team, and determine what changes you believe need to be made. You don't have to agree with all recommendations, as they are people's opinions. What I would normally do is run the workshop and discuss all the feedback. Record which feedback will be acted on, and then record which feedback will not be acted on. The results of this should then be presented to the steering committee to get their endorsement of the recommendations.

If the changes materially alter the set of hypotheses and the services being proposed in the digital utility roadmap, then you will also need to revisit your narrative to make sure it accurately reflects the changes you have made. You will also need to re-engage the stakeholder representatives to ensure they have an updated understanding and can provide feedback. This is an iterative process that needs to continue until there are no more material changes to be made to the set of hypotheses, the digital utility roadmap or the narrative.

That brings us to the end of Chapter 8, and the end of Step 3 in the ENERGY framework. Before we move on, here's a list of the key points discussed:

- The focus now is on stress-testing your story. If done well, you will get feedback that helps ensure your digital utility roadmap aligns with your broader company strategy and has the support of key stakeholders.
- It's important to liaise with your stakeholders, and gain their support, before you spend money on a new service.
- Leverage your stakeholder representatives to tell your story on your behalf. They will have greater credibility and are more likely to secure support.
- By meeting with your various stakeholder groups, you'll gain the necessary feedback and support, enabling you to properly evaluate each service before investing in it.
- This is an iterative process. As you incorporate feedback from your stakeholders, the set of hypotheses, the digital utility roadmap, and even the narrative may change. If any of them change significantly, you need to go through this process again.

Chapter 9:
Resource

A common mistake many of us make is to start the innovation process at the point of trying to secure funds for a specific investment. It's a fairly predictable path – one that I have been down many times – often with negative outcomes. Here's how it typically plays out: Technology vendors present their solutions to you. You buy into the story they are selling, and you secure some seed funding to run some pilots, or, in some cases, you may even present a business case to the executive in order to jump straight into a larger scale rollout. Despite early signs not being positive, you persevere, as this is now the path your organisation is on.

There was one example where I fell victim to exactly this. I was exploring energy management solutions for large commercial and industrial customers. It was a new area for me and I was trying to learn fast. I got sold on the story of artificial intelligence and the promises of what it could deliver. I did not follow my own rules, and had not mapped out the services we needed and why we needed them. The end result? A year's worth of time, money and manpower spent on a pilot project where nothing useful was learnt. Even when pilots are properly designed, you expect a percentage to never progress beyond the pilot stage. But you always expect to identify key lessons that can be carried forward to the next pilot. In this case, the solution was nowhere near ready and the team didn't have clarity on what we were trying to achieve, so no lessons were learned (other than the obvious one, which is to put the effort in upfront by understanding why you are doing something, and what you plan on doing, before you explore the technology).

It's a common pattern, but one we must break. We are getting overwhelmed by the number of innovations, the speed at which technologies are moving, and the expectations from those around us that we need to provide them with direction and certainty. However, you need to resist the temptation to spend money on the next big thing until you are clear on what you need to do, and why.

Having completed the first three steps of the ENERGY framework, you now have a roadmap of services that are to be introduced in the coming years. Some of these services first need to go through various piloting phases, others need further research, and some will be fully implemented. You will have a clear understanding of the four Ps against each service. You will also have a clear understanding of what your various stakeholder groups think about the services, and whether they are supportive.

Now you need to secure resources in the form of:

- Funding
- People
- Solutions
- Partners

In this step, I'll show you how to secure resources in all four areas, ensuring each service you introduce is set up for maximum success.

Resource 1: Funding

In order to secure funding, you need to write a business case. This is both an art and a science. It relies heavily on assumptions that can determine whether you proceed with an investment, and in what direction you should proceed. In this context, assumptions are necessary as you cannot be certain of future outcomes. For example, when you introduce smart meters, you aim to eliminate having to physically send a person to read the meter. In reality, it is impossible to remotely read 100 per cent of meters all the time. So you need to make an assumption about what percentage of meters will be read remotely. These assumptions help you calculate costs and benefits. The challenge with assumptions is that a small shift in a percentage can have a massive impact on whether a business case shows a positive return on investment. Careful consideration needs to be given at this stage. This is often where we see egos and agendas get in the way of common sense, logic, and what the data is telling us. Even where there is a positive, tangible return that appears to be black and white, and therefore a no-brainer, it is not always the case.

Where a service has a lot of unknowns, and where it cannot be easily justified, consider providing seed funding to run a pilot, as this has the potential to strengthen your business case.

How a pilot can strengthen your business case

Where you are introducing something completely new, a pilot may be the best way forward to test your hypotheses relating to the business models, the value proposition, the costs, the challenges, and how success will be measured. It is during these pilots that you will identify many of the obstacles. Not all of them – there are obstacles that you will only uncover as you scale out – but you will uncover enough to know if you should continue to the next step.

There have been many investments that, had I made them at scale, would have been disastrous for the organisation. Making small investments allows you to learn, course-correct, or close out altogether. For example, many of the services you want to introduce will need infrastructure that requires a large investment at scale, such as smart metering. If you have a government mandate to roll out these sorts of technologies, great. If not, you need to find the best path to start the journey. Trying to justify tens of millions of dollars to scale out smart metering is likely to be met with a lot of resistance by many internal and external stakeholder groups, unless you have data points that can show the success this will deliver.

This is where a pilot can prove useful. If you can roll out the service on a smaller scale, and present positive results to stakeholders, the project is more likely to garner the necessary support and, as a result, be a success. The flipside is that if the results are *not* positive, this is a clear sign that you still have lessons to learn, and that you should return to the drawing board before presenting a business case to secure resources for a full implementation at scale.

When trying to secure funding, be clear on why. Is it to create a baseline of services, where you have no metrics in place today? Is it to run pilot services to learn about the costs, benefits and challenges, and ultimately decide whether there is value in implementing at scale? Or is it to justify implementing the service at scale?

It is often best to bundle many of the services into a single business case. Where services logically go together, doing this avoids issues with double counting costs and benefits, especially when the services may be best implemented under the management of a single project.

Once you have a solid business case for the services you want to introduce, it's time to secure the necessary resources.

Resource 2: People

You will need to decide how these projects are to be resourced. For large-scale implementations, we often see the creation of dedicated project teams, in which people from your business partner with solution integrators and other vendors. The line-of-business operations try to backfill the day-to-day operations with contractor resources. This is a very typical model where you try to get from A to B as quickly as possible.

The introduction of certain services may be run as projects led by lines of business, and where resources continue on both operations and project work.

I have found it best to have a separate team manage the implementation of pilots, but leverage line-of-business resources. The involvement of line-of-business resources is key for a number of reasons. Most notably, if the pilot is successful and you plan to scale out, you want the buy-in and support from the lines of business that will be responsible for its operations. It is also important to involve lines of business as they know how things work today, so can highlight any issues with the new systems and processes you are testing.

Whichever model you decide on, the key is the active and early engagement of line-of-business leaders whose business areas will be impacted by the upcoming changes. You will know, from the analysis completed to date, which business units will be impacted by the implementation of the services in your roadmap. You should have engaged the leaders of these business units in the previous stage, where you evaluated your set of hypotheses, digital utility roadmap and narrative.

Assuming you have previously engaged the business unit leaders and secured support for the roadmap you have put forward, you now need to agree on how to resource the delivery of the program. If you have not engaged them, or you did and they were not supportive of your plans, then you have a problem to resolve. I have found it best to have conversations directly with the leader who is not supportive of my plans. If you fail to get their support, then you need to have a discussion with the sponsor of the program. There is a high likelihood the program will fail if a senior leader within the business does not support it.

Resource 3: Solutions

Here you need to identify which solutions will deliver the outcomes you need. This is likely to take the form of a tender, where you ask different solution vendors to bid on meeting your requirements. For a digital utility roadmap, this consists of many services to be delivered over a long period of time. Where some services are to be piloted, and others implemented at scale, I would expect to see multiple tenders. This is because you will need multiple solutions. The key to success here is early engagement of your IT architecture team.

Over the years, IT architects have had a bad rap. I know, as I used to lead a team of architects. I'll be the first to put my hand up and say we did not do ourselves any favours. Architects are often seen as the people who say no to the initiatives the business wants to move forward with, as the proposed solutions do not align with the technology standards the architects have set. I would recommend effort be spent engaging your architects early, and making them part of this journey from the start. Your architects are invaluable to this process – if they have been given the right brief, with plenty of lead time. If provided with an intimate knowledge of your proposed digital utility roadmap and vendor options, your architects can help determine how all of this needs to work together. You need to be clear on the constraints you are working under, such as time and cost. Otherwise, your architect is likely to put forward an amazing solution, but one that can never be delivered within your budget or timeframe. Avoiding your architects entirely may speed up the delivery of your project, and it may even mean your project is slightly cheaper. But in the long term, you have created a bigger headache for your organisation, as you may have selected a solution that sends you down a certain path and becomes incredibly expensive to course-correct. For these reasons, your architects should oversee a program-wide view of the technologies you are planning to invest in.

Taking the time to work with your architects and come up with a set of requirements for each new service – which allow you to leverage existing capabilities where it makes sense, and introduce new ones where it doesn't – is key. Allow me to explain why this is so important, using a real-life example.

I had an experience with IT architects when I piloted smart metering. The meter data would be read remotely with a new application, but would then feed into our existing application architecture. The data went from the new application into the existing meter data management platform, where it was validated and – where necessary – corrected. The data was then fed into the customer information system, so a bill could be created and sent to the customer. This is a very common approach, known as a three-tier architecture. We had engaged our IT architects early, and they had advised that the longer term plan was to remove the meter data management system from the process, as it would deliver performance improvements and cost savings. However, they accepted that had we included this in our pilot, the costs would have been too great and the pilot never would have got off the ground. Once the pilot was completed and the full implementation commenced, the requirement to remove the meter data management system from the process was incorporated. In this example, the early and effective engagement of the IT architects meant the pilot project was able to achieve the most cost-effective outcome to deliver on its pilot objectives, while the broader organisation objectives were met by ensuring we factored in the new architecture as we came to implement at scale.

Resource 4: Partners

We have all made the mistake of partnering with vendors when we do not have a clear view of what we want and why. We get convinced this third party has the experience and expertise that we do not, so we allow them to take the reins. We absolutely need a partner ecosystem to help us deliver many of the outcomes we're striving for, but, as I've stressed throughout this book, we must be clear on why we are introducing a new service, and the outcomes we want to achieve as a result. Only then should we enlist external partners to help us achieve those outcomes.

It must be remembered that, no matter what third-party solution providers are saying to you, they have three simple goals:

- They want you to buy their service or product at the highest margin possible.
- They want you to use their solutions as much as possible.
- They want to be with you for the long term.

I am generalising, but we have all been there in one way or another. A vendor is no different from any other business. They get a foot in the door and, if they are smart, they build a relationship with you. Before you know it, you are buying more services and products from them than you initially planned to. This is not a bad thing, providing these services and products deliver what you need, and don't prevent you from introducing other services as part of your roadmap. But there are some things to be wary of.

A common mistake I see organisations make involves deciding which smart meters to purchase. This is a fast-emerging space, for example, recently we have seen smart meters incorporate edge processing (also referred to as distributed intelligence). Basically, it means there is computing power placed at the edge of a network so analysis can be performed, decisions made, and actions taken without having to send the data back to the central systems. Rather than capturing data from a meter every fifteen to thirty minutes – before sending it back to the utility three or four times a day, and then waiting for it to process overnight – the meter is collecting data at sub-second intervals and can perform analysis while the data is in the meter. If it detects irregular patterns (signalling energy theft, power quality issues, outages, and so on), it can alert the utility. However, in the many conversations I have had in recent years, edge processing is still a poorly understood concept. People get it mixed up with the ability to remotely configure the meter or provide a patch update. These are far from similar. Due to the lack of understanding of the value of this, and with vendors that don't have the capability playing down its value, we see decisions revert back to purchasing what I consider basic smart meters. I am seeing similar issues emerge with network communications, people are confused as to what radio technology standards to adopt. Being clear on what services you are likely to require in the future will allow you to identify the right solutions, as well as the right partners to help you implement them.

No one partner will deliver all the services on your roadmap, so you need to put processes in place to ensure you're always choosing the right partners. You achieve this by being clear on what services you are planning to introduce, when, and why.

You can ensure the partners in the ecosystem work well together by setting out expectations from the start. Namely, that success will be measured collectively and not by an individual vendor. For example, if three different vendors provide solutions to get an electricity bill to a customer, then I want to see evidence that those three partners are working together to deliver the outcomes I want. You must avoid situations where partner A is pointing the finger at partner B. The only organisation that loses in that scenario is you, the utility.

That brings us to the end of Chapter 9, and the end of Step 4 in the ENERGY framework. Before we move on, here's a list of the key points discussed:

- We are overwhelmed by the number of innovations, the speed at which the technologies are moving, and the expectations of those around us. However, you must resist the temptation to spend money on the "next big thing".

- Rather, you need to be clear on what you want to achieve, and why. Then secure resources in four key areas: Funding, people, solutions and partners.

- Where you don't have a baseline set of metrics for a service, you cannot identify improvement opportunities. Consider funding a small initiative to create a baseline.

- Where a service has a lot of unknowns, and where it cannot be easily justified, consider providing seed funding to run a pilot, as this has the potential to strengthen your business case for a full-scale implementation.

- You will need to decide how these projects are to be resourced. The key is the active and early engagement of line-of-business leaders whose business areas will be impacted by the upcoming changes.

- You need to identify which solutions will deliver the outcomes you need. This is likely to take the form of a tender, where you ask different solution vendors to bid on meeting your requirements. The key to success here is early engagement of your IT architecture team.

- You need a partner ecosystem to help you deliver many of the outcomes you're striving for. However, you must be clear on why you are introducing a new service, and the outcomes you want to achieve as a result. Only then should you enlist external partners to help you achieve those outcomes.

Chapter 10:
Govern

At this point, we have the approval to commence the delivery of the digital utility roadmap. This will be made up of a series of initiatives. Some will focus on capturing metrics so we can create a baseline on how we perform today in certain parts of the business. Others will look to invest in pilots that will test certain services. And some will focus on implementing a service at scale to a large part of your customer base.

When things move into delivery, they become very real. There are a huge number of moving parts, and there are decisions that need to be made that some important people won't support. In fact, some key players will actively set out to change certain decisions. External events (such as the emergence of disruptive technology, or an unexpected policy change) will occur during this journey that will require you to course-correct, sometimes quite significantly. All of this requires effective governance, and that's what I intend to show you in this step – how to effectively govern the delivery of your digital utility roadmap.

Work out your governance structure

For any new program you introduce, you should ensure you have very structured internal governance in place. A steering committee – made up of the line-of-business executives, as well as those responsible for public affairs, people and culture, legal, and so on – is essential. The purpose of the steering committee is to help decisions get made. In the earlier stages of the program, this could relate to endorsing the recommended set of hypotheses, the digital utility roadmap and the narrative. The steering committee is also involved in the development of the stakeholder engagement plan, and decides which stakeholder feedback should be taken on board, and which should not.

The steering committee also helps make decisions that mitigate risks, resolve issues, and determine course corrections. The steering committee must have its eye firmly on the desired outcomes of the investments, so it can ask questions to ensure everything is on track. The role of the steering committee is invaluable; it must be able to ask the tough questions that may eventually lead to an investment being stopped.

During the early stages of implementing the ENERGY framework, the steering committee is focused on development of the roadmap, justification of the investments, and gaining support from stakeholders. It should be chaired by the Chief Executive Officer, Chief Operations Officer or Chief Customer Officer. Basically, the person who has complete oversight of the company, or at the very least someone who oversees operations or customer relations. Committee members typically include heads of strategy, public affairs, human resources, finance and procurement. Depending on the agenda, various senior managers from lines of business would also be invited to attend.

As the program moves into delivery, the steering committee is now focused on execution and benefit realisation. While the membership of the steering committee would remain much the same, you would now see senior managers (from the lines of business that will be directly impacted by the services being introduced) take a more permanent role on the committee.

Understanding the senior executives who will have the most influence over the program is important. If you think back to the section on stakeholder analysis in Chapter 6, influence and interest changes over time. I have had situations where, at the start of the program, trying to get some executives to attend meetings was almost impossible. As those executives woke up to the fact that the changes were going to be either an opportunity or a threat to them, suddenly they wanted to be involved in everything, revisit decisions that had already been made, and change the direction of things.

In particular, I have found the levels of interest from various stakeholders change dramatically as soon as there's a major change or breakthrough in the business. For example, we ran a demand response program with residential customers. We were trying to get them to reduce their air conditioning usage for a few hours during the hottest and most humid times of the year. When we consistently saw reductions in peak demand of fifteen to twenty per cent, we suddenly realised this was very real. We had a service that could fundamentally change the way the organisation balances supply with demand. It could mean the deferral of investment in generation infrastructure. It would now mean a totally different relationship with our customers. It meant conversations with the government over policy that needed to change. With these results, a number of the senior executives – who rarely took an interest before – started attending every steering committee meeting and giving their input on decisions that needed to be made. This is both a good thing and a bad thing. It's good because now you have senior leaders engaged and helping the program to move forward. It's bad because these executives did not take an interest earlier. As they come up to speed, they may decide to challenge the original set of hypotheses, the digital utility roadmap or the narrative. This can create an enormous amount of extra work, as you now need to gain support from previously uninterested senior executives.

In addition to a steering committee, I have found establishing a second committee – or, to be precise, an advisory board made up of well-respected external professionals – can help address even the most sensitive issues. The external executives should be representatives from some of your key external stakeholder groups such as local academia and industry bodies. While everyone has a bias based on beliefs that have been formed over the years, an external group can offer a different perspective; a view that does not consider the internal objectives of the organisation.

The importance of the steering committee and advisory board cannot be understated. The representatives of these groups must take an active role. With the delivery teams so focused on the detail, it is essential that performance metrics are reviewed, that tough questions are asked, and that timely decisions are made. The digital utility roadmap will take you on a transformational journey, so you need to ensure that whoever's steering the ship is 100 per cent on board and actively involved.

Support your start-up team

In Chapter 4, we talked about the need to think like a start-up, and even set up a start-up-esque team. You should encourage your team to adopt a start-up mentality, and this includes the steering committee. When governing the implementation of a multimillion-dollar project into your mainstream business, you need to eliminate risks to create certainty of outcome. When running pilot projects, your steering committee needs to encourage a higher degree of risk taking. As you learn, you will course-correct, and therefore you may change the direction of the pilot. Steering committee members need to support the different mindset and approach of those running pilots to test services, as compared to those implementing services at scale.

With start-ups, it's about challenging the logic behind certain directions being taken, as there is rarely much data to support decisions. Hence the need for a pilot. There is rarely a lot of money available, so it is about finding smart ways to deliver outcomes. Course correction is not a sign of failure – quite the opposite. It means you have learned something valuable that now needs to be applied, so you need to pivot. Levels of risk acceptance will be much higher. The notion of perfection is the enemy of good start-ups. Getting things out to the market quickly is more important than getting everything in place before going to market.

For us in utilities, this is all a bit confronting. For 100 years, it has been drilled into us that all risk must be eliminated to ensure safe and reliable supply. The problem is that this risk-averse culture has permeated its way into every part of our businesses. As an industry, we are rewarded when we toe the line and do not challenge the norm. As a member of a governance board overseeing a team instructed to innovate and find ways to use energy data to deliver customer value, you need to show that the pilot team are supported. Why is this important? Because mistakes will happen. Also, only a low percentage of pilots will ever go beyond pilot phase. Of the twenty-plus smart energy pilot projects I have overseen, about a quarter have made it to mainstream production.

The type of people selected for pilots is critical. They need to be highly energetic, keen to challenge the status quo, and comfortable with ambiguity. They need to accept that they do not know everything, and be keen to learn.

The team itself needs to be set up for success. They must be rewarded for identifying new opportunities, even if they go nowhere. They must be recognised for testing new ways of working, and challenging how things are done today. They must be encouraged to think outside the box and come up with creative ways to solve problems. Ultimately, you need to decide what success looks like for this team. For me, it would be twenty-five per cent of all pilot initiatives getting implemented within four years of the pilot being completed. This gives enough flexibility for the innovation team to take risks, but also a clear target to aim for.

That brings us to the end of Chapter 10, and the end of Step 5 in the ENERGY framework. Before we move on to the final step, here's a list of the key points covered:

- When you introduce a new service or program, there are a huge number of moving parts. In addition to changing levels of interest from the various people involved, external events will occur that will require you to course-correct, sometimes quite significantly. All of this requires effective governance.

- For any new programs you introduce, you should ensure you have very structured internal governance in place. A steering committee, including a designated chairperson, is essential. You should also establish an advisory board, made up of external stakeholders, to offer a different perspective.

- The steering committee's active involvement is critical to the success of this program, and should have appropriate senior representation.

- Your pilots need to be supported differently from implementations of services at scale. The team running the pilots needs to be encouraged to take more risks, challenge the status quo, and think outside the box.

Chapter 11:
Yield

By now, you should have a clear roadmap supported by your key stakeholders, both internal and external. You should have secured the necessary funding, people, solutions and partners to be part of the program. A steering committee should be in place, containing all the senior leaders impacted by your program, along with an independent advisory board made up of industry experts and local academia. You have completed all of the necessary steps to set yourself up for success. Unfortunately, it is often at this point that the wheels can come off, and all of your careful planning gets derailed (the reasons for this are explained below). In this final step in the ENERGY framework, I'll show you how to stay focused on the project – right to the very end.

Do not yield to the opinions of others

There is now a huge amount of momentum toward delivering the project. However, that's not always a good thing, as it means we have a tendency to lose sight of delivering the outcomes. As we go through the implementation phase of a project, we must continue to look at what the data is telling us and act on those insights. After all, some people's livelihoods will depend on these projects. We have brought in vendors and contractors, and we have seconded people from different parts of the business, giving them a new or accelerated career path. In short, there is a lot at stake – which is why the steering committee has a very active role to play during the delivery phase. All too often, I see the steering committee focus on the successful completion of the project, not the successful delivery of specific outcomes. Earlier in the book, I talked about the 'canary in the coalmine' concept. There are often lead indicators that act as an early warning system, signalling whether the project needs to course-correct, or even stop altogether. In these situations, we must not yield to people's opinions – to carry on in a certain direction – if the data does not support it.

Let me give you an example. I recall a project a few years ago that had buy-in from all senior executives. Halfway through, a very senior member left and their replacement stepped in. It soon became obvious that this project was heading in a direction the new senior executive did not want to take and, within weeks, the project was closed out altogether. A couple of years later, the organisation headed down the same path it had originally mapped out. It had essentially lost a couple of valuable years by yielding to one person's opinion rather than looking at what the data was telling it.

Hopefully, this example highlights why you should not yield to the opinions of others. Take opinions on board, but take them for what they are – opinions. Which often come with a bias, whether intentional or otherwise. Before making decisions to continue, stop or change course, look at what the lead indicators are telling you. Don't look at just the performance of the project – that will send you and your decisions in the wrong direction. Look at whether the project looks set to deliver the customer value you expect. This, after all, is your ultimate goal.

Check the health of your canary

This leads me to my next point: Regularly check the health of your 'canary', or lead indicators. Your primary metrics are the most important indicators to monitor. Is your net promoter score trending in the right direction? Is your cost to serve decreasing? Is the profitability of your customers increasing? In addition to these primary metrics, it is valuable to look at your innovation team's output. Are they increasing the percentage of pilots that move to full-scale implementation? Is the impact of the pilots that move to full-scale implementation delivering increasing value to your customers and organisational performance?

You are placing a lot of importance on the canary, so make sure your canary is healthy. Looking at the wrong indicators, or the wrong data, may result in some very regrettable decisions. Adoption of behind-the-meter technology is happening so fast that we are not yet sure which opportunities we should take advantage of, and what threats we need to defend against. I believe the best we can do is build flexibility into our businesses and prepare to course-correct – regularly. To do this, we need to work closely with our IT architects and ensure they are working to the same set of principles as the rest of the business. For years, their principles were based on eradicating duplication of processes and systems, leveraging standards, and consolidating as many technologies as possible. These principles led to investments in monolithic applications that were great at reducing cost to serve, but awful in terms of flexibility and bringing products to market quickly. With technology at the heart of the digital utility, you must bring your IT architects on this journey and get them to help you build flexibility into the IT architecture.

We know home automation is happening, we know transportation is becoming electrified, and we know adoption of distributed generation and storage will continue to rise. We know peer-to-peer energy trading is emerging, and we know edge computing is maturing. There is a lot we know. However, in most areas, traditional data points would still suggest: 'Don't invest in them as they will not yield a return.' This simply means your data points are dated and wrong. I understand it is incredibly scary to look at the lead indicators and realise your organisation needs to transform. It is even scarier when you don't know what direction this transformation will take. So, start small, and build an ecosystem that embraces innovation, and that allows you to test and learn. Build a capability that allows you to course-correct. Most of all, build a culture that looks at lead indicators, and is bold enough to take action on what those indicators are telling you so you do not yield to the opinions of those who may not be sufficiently informed, or may have reasons to resist change.

This has to be supported from the very top. Executives who punish people for making mistakes will create a culture where issues and new ideas are buried. Everyone will keep their heads down and deliver exactly what is asked, even if they know it won't deliver the right outcomes. Executives must encourage and reward those who are prepared to make mistakes – so long as they learn from them. People must feel comfortable speaking out and challenging decisions that have been made. This does not mean decisions should get overturned, but we should encourage concerns to be put on the table so they can be discussed and addressed.

Revisit and revise

Having completed all six steps in the ENERGY framework, you will have started to implement a series of initiatives that leverage energy data. Some of these initiatives will simply be the implementation of technologies to start capturing data to create a baseline. Others will be small-scale pilots to test consumer behaviour. And there will also be some initiatives that are being rolled out to the majority, if not all, of your customer base.

The important thing to remember is that this process never ends. You need to constantly check you have included all the necessary stakeholders. You also need to constantly check the sentiment of those stakeholders. Has their position changed? Do they now have a greater level of interest or influence, for whatever reason?

Execution of your roadmap may be going well, but is it still valid? Have there been new competitors entering your market? Are new technologies making earlier decisions obsolete? Are there policy changes that look like disrupting your plans?

The ENERGY framework should not be thought of as a one-off exercise. In fact, the ENERGY framework should not even be thought of as an exercise you constantly repeat, starting back at Step 1 when you complete Step 6. You may be working on all steps simultaneously. Developing a business case for one service, while implementing another. Updating your stakeholder engagement plan, while talking to stakeholders about services you are planning to deliver.

This may appear complex and messy; it is because it reflects real life. But once you've worked through the framework once, you'll find it a lot easier to juggle different steps – for different services – simultaneously.

Before I share my final thoughts with you, here are the key points to remember from Chapter 11:

- As you go through the implementation phase of a project, you must continue to look at what the data is telling you, and act on those insights.

- There are often lead indicators that act as an early warning system, signalling whether the project needs to course-correct, or even stop altogether. In these situations, you must not yield to people's opinions if the data does not support it.

- You are placing a lot of importance on your 'canary' (lead indicators), so make sure your canary is healthy. Looking at the wrong indicators, or the wrong data, may result in some very regrettable decisions.

- The ENERGY framework should not be thought of as a one-off exercise. It should not even be thought of as an exercise you repeat in linear fashion. You may work on all steps – for different services – simultaneously.

Conclusion:
Utility of the future

A few years have passed since you completed the ENERGY framework for the first time. You have the foundational technologies in place, such as a demand response management system, advanced metering infrastructure, perhaps even updates to your outage management and demand management systems. Your focus initially has been to tackle the low-hanging fruit. Reduce your costs by minimising non-technical loss, introduce remote-reading meters, and eliminate estimated reads and the enquiries that relate to this. You have not yet scaled out smart meters to everyone – this is a long journey. One that has included upgrades to your customer information system and your meter data management system. You have invested in upgrading your analytical capabilities, with regard to both people and technologies. A whole bunch of other systems and business processes have changed. In fact, your entire organisational structure has changed. You have a 24/7 operation managing the capture of energy data so you can deliver the various services.

You have started to run demand response pilots to see if customers will reduce their consumption during the handful of hottest hours each year. You are exploring whether consumers will change their consumption behaviour with time-based and demand-based pricing, so you can see if this improves your overall load factor. You are also running pilots to better understand how your demand response management system may be able to communicate with the latest smart home hubs from the likes of Apple, Amazon and Google.

There is a long way to go, but you are confident you are heading in the right direction. You finally have the time to sit back and think: What next?

Next stop: Smart cities

We are at the start of a transformation in our industry. This transformation is a good thing. It's moving us all towards a more sustainable planet. A planet that we should want to leave to our children in a better state than it was handed to us. As a utility executive, you are in an enviable position. You can make the decisions that place you at the heart of this journey. The journey I'm talking about, specifically, is the rise of smart cities.

Electric utilities are the heartbeat of a city. The generation, transmission and distribution of electricity is not called critical infrastructure without reason. Every aspect of our lives today is driven by electricity. For those of us who embrace the challenge of collaborating with consumers to help with the adoption of behind-the-meter technologies, for those of us who expose their energy data to third parties, and for those who partner with parallel industries to explore ways to collaborate and deliver holistic solutions for our customers, there are amazing opportunities to become a central part of the journey in building smart and sustainable cities.

We, as an industry, have an amazing opportunity to be part of a much larger ecosystem. We don't have to directly compete in those verticals. We just need to collaborate with others. Think about the value in the energy data you hold, and what this will do for policymakers, academics and business owners. Sharing this data will open up possibilities our individual utilities, and even our industry as a whole, may have never discovered.

Think about the infrastructure we have in place. We have the ability to securely and efficiently capture energy data from electricity meters. What if we provided this service to other service providers, such as gas, water, waste, and so on? If we don't want to perform the service for them, what about leasing access to our infrastructure? This provides our industry with additional income, which can be used to reinvest in further improving our performance, or simply helping to reduce the electricity rates our customers pay. Remember, our partner industries of gas and water are not as advanced as us when it comes to the introduction of smart grids, smart meters, and behind-the-meter technologies. We have a lot we can offer our partner industries.

Your driver is to ensure your utility is a central part of the journey to a smart and sustainable city, where consumers come to your platform for services, and where other businesses come to your platform to sell to others. All city-wide services would leverage the two-way data-flow facilitated by this platform. Whether that be waste, transportation, gas, electricity, home security – the list goes on. You would start with your target niche, which is the electricity consumer, and then grow over time. There are a number of start-ups, as well as established players, looking to enter this market. We have an advantage here, because we already have infrastructure in place to capture energy data. We are already capturing the energy data and processing it, even if it's just for billing. We have first-mover advantage. Launching a platform that makes this data available, and encouraging the establishment of a partner ecosystem to offer a range of applications and services that leverage this data, will draw more and more people to the platform.

If you're not sure what I mean by this, think about Amazon. It always had the vision to be the world's online store, but it started with a niche: Books. They were easy to sell online, easy to package, and easy to distribute. Gradually over the past decade, Amazon has moved into many other verticals and is challenging almost every area of retail, including energy.

I suggest we take a similar approach, starting with what we know best – electricity – and then extending to other verticals gradually. We don't have to be responsible for collecting all the data. We just need to partner with those who do, so we can expose it to third-party service providers. There is enormous value in exposing electricity, gas, water and waste data to third party service providers.

We are entering an era where we need to think big and be bold. Due to advancements in technologies, we have the luxury of thinking big but executing incrementally, allowing us to course-correct as we learn.

You have three choices:

- Go it alone and develop a platform that manages the two-way flow of electricity data and electrons.

- Form partnerships so, collectively, you manage the two-way flow of various data and various energy sources.

- Ignore the whole smart city move and continue to work in an isolated fashion.

I know which one I would go for. What about you?

Acknowledgements

To my children, including the bell pepper. You are the reason that drives me to help find ways to reduce the impact we all have on the environment, so you grow up in a world not threatened by climate change.

To Phil Stone – you have always been there to listen to my crazy ideas, challenge my thinking, and help me shape them into something that delivers value.

To Andrew Griffiths and the entire KPI community, who have helped me publish this book. Your framework and ongoing support has provided me with the confidence to write the many more books I still have inside me.

To Jacqui Pretty and the team at Grammar Factory, especially my editor Michelle Hammond – you have transformed my book into something that I am truly proud of. When I received your first edit, culling twenty per cent of my book, I was in a state of shock. After reading your revisions, though, it was clear I was in the hands of professionals and I have enjoyed the entire journey. Thank you.

Most importantly to my wife, Claire. Without you I would never have had the courage to follow my dreams. You are an inspiration to me every day. I love you.

About the author

Wayne is the founder of The Chapel Group, a consulting company created in 2015 to help utilities use energy data to increase customer value and deliver business growth.

Wayne's belief is simple: There is increasing consumer adoption of behind-the-meter technologies such as rooftop solar, electric vehicles, battery storage and the connected home. Consumers are on this journey regardless of what their utility providers do. Wayne believes that by helping utilities leverage energy data and focus more on the demand side, they can deliver services and products that position them at the heart of what is an inevitable transformation to a sustainable way of living.

Wayne's subject matter expertise comes from almost twenty years in the utility industry across Asia. In that time, Wayne has been recognised for his innovation and vision by Metering & Smart Energy International.

Wayne led Southeast Asia's first end-to-end smart metering and demand response program, which resulted in a twenty per cent reduction in peak demand, and won a series of awards across the Asia Pacific region.

Wayne is a father, a guest lecturer at the Asian Institute of Technology, and a regular contributor for many of the leading industry magazines. He is also a sought-after speaker at Asia Pacific energy conferences. *The Digital Utility* is his second book.